Dedication

To

Lestina Grant, the psychologist I most highly respect, who, in 1972, hired and guided me in consulting in the Philadelphia schools where I first consciously realized and applied Social Play techniques.

To

Emma Mobley, Ellen Berger, Sylvia Smith and in memory of Rita Nathanson, the teachers in the portable annex of Logan School, and to their students who were the first to enjoy Social Play lead by me.

To

my son, Robert, whose belief in Social Play is the inspiration for this second edition.

And to

my brother Barry Reddish, who's computer expertise and help, saved me from utter PC despair.

Also to

Beverly Houck, who along with Robert helped me form Playcorp, Inc., and who edited the manuscript.

ABOUT THE AUTHOR

Frank Aycox, teacher, therapist, recreation leader and author, grew up playing street games in Philadelphia in the early forties. Thirty years later he casually played similar games with students in a Philadelphia school as a consultant from the local Community Mental Health Center. The troubled students responded so favorably to the games that he developed a more extensive and systematic body of social games which teachers could use to cultivate positive classroom behaviors. After several years of successfully leading social games, Mr. Aycox became intrigued as to how and why the play brought about positive behavior changes in students. This book is the culmination of his discoveries, research, and experience.

Mr. Aycox spent several years as a middle school science teacher and taught Physical Education, Recreation and Leisure as a Teaching Associate at Temple University where he received a M.Ed. in Therapeutic Recreation. He worked ten years as a therapist in several inpatient agencies serving children and adolescents. Mr. Aycox was formerly Director of Expressive Arts Therapies at Northwestern Institute of Psychiatry in Fort Washington, Pennsylvania, and is a past Board Member of the Eastern Cooperative Recreation School.

Mr. Aycox leads seminars and inservices on the theory and practice of Social Play for family service, community mental health agencies, schools and colleges over wide areas of the country. He has trained recreational specialists of the YMCA, and has conducted assembly programs for hundreds of schools throughout the United States.

Mr. Aycox's background in teaching, recreation and therapy is a unique blend of knowledge and experience which has enabled him to create a social, cultural, play system that he feels is the perfect social skills curriculum for use in the contemporary school.

In 1995 Mr. Aycox founded Playcorp, Inc., a consulting firm that applies Social Play techniques not only to the education process but to the work place culture of businesses and social service agencies.

GAMES WE SHOULD PLAY
IN
SCHOOL

A Revealing Analysis of the Social Forces in the Classroom
and
What To Do About Them

A Proven Social Skills Curriculum

That Includes Over 75 Interactive, Fun Social Games

<u>2nd Edition</u>

by

Frank Aycox, M.Ed.

EDITOR
Frank Alexander

TEXT ARTIST
Russ McKinny

Published
by
Front Row Experience

NOTICE
The information
contained in this book
is true and complete
to the best of our knowledge.
It is offered with no guarantees
on the part of the author or Front Row Experience.
The author and publisher disclaim all liability
in connection with the use of this book.

Published
by
Front Row Experience
540 Discovery Bay Blvd.
Discovery Bay, CA 94514-9454

CONTENTS

Preface

Introduction 1
The Fundamentals Of Learning.............................2
Two Extremes 3
A Balanced Approach 3
Challenge To Educators 3

Chapter 1
UNDERSTANDING *SOCIAL PLAY*

What Is *Social Play*...5
Recognizing School As A Social Institution 6
Social Play Goals 7

Chapter 2
WHY *SOCIAL PLAY?*

Children's Developmental Needs 9
Children's Social Needs 13
Self-Esteem At School 18
Cooperative Learning 19

Chapter 3
MAKING THE SYSTEM WORK

Leadership Philosophy 20
Leadership Techniques 20
The Techniques...21

Chapter 4
BEHAVIOR PROBLEMS IN THE SCHOOLS

Ten Classroom Problems and *Social Play* Remedies 23
For A Better Understanding Of Student/Teacher Problems 29
The Teacher and *Social Play* 30

Chapter 5
THE GAMES

Play—More Than Fun 33
The Social Game—A Special Kind of Play 33
A Big Wind Blows! 35
Airport 36
Alibi 37
Alphabet Race 39
Alphabet Volleyball 41
Balloon Burst Relay 42
Bird, Beast, Or Fish! 43
Broom Hockey 44
Bull In The Ring 45
Caboose Dodgeball 46
Catch A Smile 48
Chain Pantomime 49
Chosen 51
Circle Kho 52
Coffee Pot 53
Coin Relay 54
Colored Squares 56
Come Along 58
Dzien Dobry 60
Elbow Tag 62
El Tigre 64
Elephant And Giraffe 66
Fibbing 68
Fire On The Mountain 69
Front To Front 71
Fruit Salad 73
Go Around 75

Group Buzz 77
Guard The Chair 79
Guess The Leader 80
How Do You Like Your Neighbor? 81
Howdy Neighbor 83
Human Tic-Tac-Toe 85
I'm Going To California 87
I'm Thinking Of A Word That Rhymes With 88
In Plain View 90
In The Manner Of The Adverb 91
Jerusalem Jericho 92
Jump Stick Relay 94
Kangaroo Relay 96
Last Couple Stoop 97
Lemonade 99
Line Tug Of War 101
Manito 103
Pass A Smile 105
Predicament 106
Pressure Nouns 107
Pris 109
Quick Draw 111
Quick Line Up 112
Quick Numbers 114
Rescue Relay 116
Scavenger Hunt 117
Singing Geography 119
Singing Hot And Cold 120
Steal The Dog's Bone 121
Steeple Chase 123
Stride Ball 125
Swat 126
Swedish Baseball 128
The Parlour Game (Charades) 129
Thread The Needle 131
Tire Pull 132
Touch 133
Twenty One 134
Up Jenkins 135
Vegetarianism 137
Wave The Ocean 138

Who Am I? 139
Zip Zap! 140

Appendix

Letters To The Author—What The Children Say 141
What Teachers Say About *Social Play* 149
Suggested Reading 150
Index Of Games 151

PREFACE

Social Play is a noncommercial, cultural art form that is effective in overcoming isolation and alienation of people. The most valuable contribution of *Social Play* is realized when applied to the contemporary school because it is through its practice that 'good' social behavior is learned by children.

The professional preparation of teachers does not adequately develop a child appropriate social skills curriculum that results in children learning social behavior. The teacher preparation curriculum teaches theoretical concepts of child development (Erikson, Piaget, etc.) and stresses looking at children as individuals outside their social environment. This emphasis does not equip teachers to respond to or understand children in complex social groupings. Because the course work fails to deal with children as *social beings* and fails to translate abstract concepts into concrete, practical classroom activities, many teachers attempt to enforce *adult* behavioral criteria on children without an analysis as to whether these criteria are developmentally appropriate or even *possible* for their students.

This books is designed to help fill this void.

Children do not volunteer to attend school and mandatory attendance does not ensure willing students nor does it guarantee that students will have the necessary social behaviors either. However, schools must meet the social needs and teach the social skills necessary for student learning. These needs and skills are determined by the children's developmental stage, their socioeconomic environment, and their emotional state. If the children's social needs are ignored by their school, antagonistic (but avoidable) struggling takes place between peers and teachers. When this kind of school environment exists, learning fails because teachers and students put their energy into struggling over issues of control and discipline.

It is my experience that optimum learning takes place when social relationships are positive. Positive relationships are developed when adults (parents, teachers and administrators) work cooperatively to provide educational facilities, personnel and programs which consistently meet the needs of children. Schools are humane when parents and school leaders set and enforce proper limits and guidelines for children, when teachers do the same in the classroom, and adults in the home, and all adults provide proper role models. Taken together this creates an environment which allows children to cooperate with all levels of the adult community, especially school.

However, if the community expects and demands behaviors from its children which are higher than their maturation level, fail to provide proper role models, or fail to set limits and guidelines, they are placing barriers in the path of the children's development. These barriers have dire implications for the future. Children frequently write letters to the author (see appendix) in which they reveal thoughts and feelings stimulated through the SP (*Social Play*) experience. A fifth grader wrote, "....I had fun playing

1

all those games, but we were bad. *We didn't act like adults!*" (My emphasis, FA.)

Children learn social skills through experiencing life, making wrong choices and being corrected under the guidance of caring adults. These interactions shape the behavioral lives of children so they make better decisions, internalize rules, and attain higher levels of self control. If adults fail to provide the necessary structured environment and ignore the children's needs, the children become distrustful of adults, and acting out behavior becomes their way of expressing being upset with social instability. ***Mischievousness** is the child's way of getting around inconsistent and arbitrary adult rules. Telling a child how not to act is the same as telling him to do the act.* The gain a child feels from misbehaving is the thrill of not getting caught. Good adult leadership structures the environment so that "getting over" provides little gain and it is cooperation that is desired and rewarded. The games in this book create an environment and structure where positive social learning is possible in school.

The Fundamentals Of Learning

Are reading, writing and arithmetic skills the real fundamentals of the schooling process? When the community has uniform social mores, stable family structures and nurturing adults, the three R's do form the basis of an educational system. However, when children grow up in conditions of social, economic and racial instability, they fail to respond to an educational system that expects them to be ready to deal with learning issues alone. This happens because children enter the school system relatively unsocialized, spending the years from birth to school entry in a home where he or she is treated as an individual in a hierarchy, not as a peer. Given a lack of uniform social rules in the community at large, the child will not acquire the social behaviors necessary to sit in a class of thirty children and handle the stimulation that comes from so many peers. *Needy children cannot postpone their emotional needs to achieve the intellectual performance desired by teachers.*

What takes place in many classrooms is social anarchy, a situation where the three R's carry little weight. Because millions of American students lack the necessary social supports (stable families, wholesome communities, or adequate wealth) to maintain emotional stability, they often start school without receiving enough nurturing and attention. When this happens to a child he or she does not mature sufficiently to handle the stimulation in the classroom. Instead of arriving at school ready to advance to the next level of social maturity, the child comes with attention deficits and behaves in an attention demanding way. The classroom dynamics then become a struggle among children who are acting out in competition over the available attention a teacher can give. The teacher, who is in an overwhelming situation, reacts negatively in an attempt to suppress the acting out children. This reaction sparks the classical antagonistic struggle between child and school. The most needy children act out the most in a desperate quest to have their attention needs met and soon other children surmise that the misbehaving child gets more of the teacher's attention and they too act out. This results in social anarchy in the classroom. It should be noted that some children suffer attention and other deficits severe enough that they become impaired. SP provides excellent therapeutic intervention in special education classes too.

The key to dealing with social anarchy is understanding the social development and social needs of children. Trying to suppress a child's needs does not work, because if a need is not met, aberrant behavior results. Exhortation, authoritarianism, isolation, and punishment fail to meet needs and set in motion a series of interactions that are destructive and counterproductive to all parties. What has to be employed are methods that meet social and emotional needs, that allow children to develop positive social behaviors and internalized self control. Only when this happens, is optimum learning possible for school children.

Two Extremes

Current practices which suppress children's drives to meet their needs rarely succeed, including the following two approaches which are in widespread use. One model relies on teachers being very strict and very authoritarian in an attempt to maintain *external* control over students. When a teacher of sufficient will dominates a group of children in this way it *appears* that the children are well behaved. But the 'good' behavior is unstable and temporary. When released from that teacher's control (going to the library, attending art or music classes, or having a substitute teacher), the children revert to social anarchy, acting out and testing limits. In addition, come Sunday evening, children with overly strict teachers become anxious and unhappy about returning to school Monday morning.

Being too lenient and lacking sufficient organization, rules and limits is the other approach that results in destructive relationships. Basically the overly lax approach gives children a voice in making or sabotaging decisions in matters that are not appropriate for them. This approach became the vogue in the sixties, when the mistaken idea that lack of structure was "freeing up" educational energy and humanizing school. But this approach ignored the fundamental issues of student social development and classroom social stability. The open classroom movement of the sixties ushered in the extremely individualistic "do-your-own-thing" philosophy. Children were expected to function under too much stimulation, make choices adults should make, and behave on a higher level than they were able to. Some open classrooms still exist, but it is no longer a popular form of school organization; it has been replaced in many areas by a more strict but not more socially effective "back to basics" movement.

A Balanced Approach

The purpose of this book is to provide two things: 1) practical activities that help students learn positive social behaviors, and 2) a method whereby teachers get to understand their students in a broader social context (play vastly expands the environment!). Armed with this information teachers can adopt approaches that do not ignore their students' needs and can organize the school program in a manner to meet them. Only then will children react more favorably to school. They will be less antagonistic, more cooperative, happier and more capable of learning. Teachers will no longer view their students as "bad" or incapable of self-control and learning. Given these changes, the school community will be a more youthful, relaxed, pleasant place.

Challenge To Educators

Educators are being thrust by history to demonstrate leadership in the current battle to save a faltering educational system, and in essence, our children. The issue is, will families support educational and cultural values or antisocial commercial ones? In the past sixty years, our communities and youth have been harmed by hot and cold wars. Children do not respond to education when their communities are perilous, their schools disorderly and disrespectful, and their parents and teachers fail to maintain a culturally rich heritage based on reading, art, dance, games, dramatics, and expressive writing. Progress in education cannot take place if a commercial, violent, pop culture dominates the classroom or when home environments are culturally and intellectually debasing. Teachers cannot be blamed if Johnny doesn't learn when they have no input in establishing the content of the mass culture (for example, what's on and how much TV is watched). When the cultural environment is opposed to education, teachers usually lose the struggle. They suffer, children suffer and whole communities suffer.

Positive changes are urgently needed to halt the deteriorating social conditions that affect young people—the dangers of drugs, racism, lack of jobs and unsafe schools. There is little chance of making positive changes without teachers playing a prominent role. This book attempts to help by offering a play based social skills curriculum which leads to a better understanding of the social needs and behavioral dynamics of children.

Nothing is more important for our nation than accomplishing the highest of human goals—a peaceful, flourishing, and enlightened society, and the only real link to such a future is raising and educating healthy and happy children in all neighborhoods.

Frank Aycox, M.Ed.
Philadelphia, Pennsylvania

Chapter 1
UNDERSTANDING *SOCIAL PLAY*

What Is *Social Play?*

Social Play is a cultural art form. It is leading a group in a series of games, so that individuals experience, learn and develop positive social attitudes and skills. The games are introduced sequentially so that more advanced social behavior is required as the play progresses. The process fashions a non-threatening, fun experience in social learning. These experiences build into a reserve of social trust that helps propel the group forward, enabling it to accomplish its tasks.

Social Play quickly sets individuals at ease by spontaneously breaking down social barriers and circumventing socially inhibiting defense mechanisms. *Social Play* removes the responsibility of initiating social interaction from the individual, who can be shy and lack the ability to structure interactions comfortably, and places it on the entire social group and its leader. Through this procedure every group member becomes actively drawn into interpersonal interaction.

The *Social Play* system encourages cooperation, harnesses competition, shapes group identity, and fosters group allegiance. *Social Play* can help overcome racial and ethnic prejudices, and transform negative group tension into tolerance, caring, and mutual support.

Social Play games have social content. This means, they must be problem solved in an interactive manner. They have a minimum of rules that must be made clear to all players. The games range from simple to complex, active to quiet, rough to intimate, and at the same time can be dramatic, musical, or intellectual.

External rewards are to be avoided in *Social Play* sessions. If focus is placed on trophies, prizes, or being "number one," children cannot fully appreciate the unfolding discovery, the intrinsic value of the moments that add up to a feeling of fun. When a child fails to win a prize he feels disappointed, frustrated, and angry with himself and resentful of others. The central aim in conducting *Social Play* is to structure the environment and relationships so that children have positive, spontaneous, and enjoyable times with their classmates and teachers. A good *Social Play* session will demonstrate that the best prize is being appreciated and accepted by the people close to us. This type of reward is never on a shelf collecting dust, but shines in one's memory.

Social Play has magical qualities. The first one is creating new social environments simply by establishing the rules of a game to be played. The magic continues as the players gain new experiences transcending those allowed in their normal environment. Although the new experiences are artificial (play derived) they are real and effect the players' lives *after* the game. The changes in individual behavior and group spirit can be astoundingly positive!

To attain optimum benefits of *Social Play*, the leader must be skillful and sensitive. She must not destroy the magic by being over controlling or not allowing the players to problem solve on their own. The leader has to be fun loving, positive, and display good leadership control. She cannot unwittingly reinforce competition, or unconsciously encourage reckless actions that endanger players. She cannot believe in superiority theories, nor value people more for their performance than for their personalities. If done well, *Social Play* appears to be easy and simple, but it is not. Leading children in the socially interactive realm, in a highly individualistic and fiercely competitive society, is a demanding task and requires a serious attitude.

Recognizing School As A Social Institution

School is basically a social institution. This is for two reasons: one, state law mandates that children attend; and two, school is where the second stage of a child's social development takes-place (in our culture this social function is unique to school). During this important *second* stage of social development, the monopoly of the family as a socializing agent comes to an end, and children must learn to relate to peers and non-parental adults. If this crucial phase of socialization is neither understood nor competently handled, children can develop life long antisocial behaviors and society ultimately suffers.

A realistic concept of education must realize that socialization skills are fundamental to the learning process. Children hardly ever suspend their emotional needs in order to complete cognitive tasks. To learn academic subjects, or work skills, the emotional health of a child and hence the quality of their social relationships must be in some semblance of adjustment. Anthropological studies show that humans developed their supreme cognitive level through an intensely social life-style, and that language originated because cooperation was crucial to survival.

Other Effects On Students' Behavior Due To A Socialization Breakdown
Increased feelings of alienation; drugs and alcohol abuse (used as self medication); attraction to cults and hate groups (they seem like a good family); running away from home; vandalism and suicide.

Unfortunately for students, many educational institutions have somewhat lost sight of the importance of their socialization role. Children sit in classrooms for months, not getting to know one another. Children report to the author that they "have fun" in activities where they get to exchange personal information like birth place and dates, favorites, pet peeves, and items of pride (see appendix). There presently exists in many schools a highly alienated form of student friendship, that of being "friends" in school and *never* meeting outside school.

Activities of a "getting-to-know-you" nature are rare in classroom routines due to several reasons. One, teachers feel pressure to produce results in the academic areas without realizing that good academic performance relates to good classroom social order. Two, they assume that spending long periods of time in the classroom will automatically result in students getting to know one another. Not so.

When in close proximity *without* a means of becoming acquainted, people act suspicious and critical—hardly the basis for being friendly.

School systems across the nation are rife with violence, vandalism, assaults on teachers, and a general lack of cooperation and respect among students. Many student bodies contain powerful cliques which function by rejecting and "putting down" others. Racial segregation, an extreme form of conscious antisocial rejection, still goes on in thousands of school districts across the nation. These situations occur because students lack integration into friendly and familiar class groupings. Introducing students to each other through *Social Play* techniques provides a viable solution to these vexing school problems.

The issue confronting school leaders is recognizing that the problems of youth are fundamentally of a social nature, usually the result of a breakdown in their families and communities. School is often the *only* stable place in a student's life. Advances in the quality of school life will happen when teaching staffs understand children's social needs and wholeheartedly make the effort to organize classrooms and entire schools in a way that meets them. When school is a socially sound community for students, their capacity for learning will be high. Their learning potential will far surpass schools that ignore the social basis of their problems and try to force children to respond positively in a negative environment.

Social Play is a process that provides real and essential experiences for children to shed negative behaviors and learn constructive ways to relate to classmates. It also makes it possible for teachers to observe these changes in behavior to better understand their students as social beings capable of positive attitudinal and behavioral changes. *Social Play* can help make the socialization process a conscious and attainable goal for teachers and do it in a medium natural for children—*here-and-now* play.

Social Play Goals

Social Play meets social needs. It counters the negative effects of the onslaught of antisocial ideas and attitudes that children absorb in their daily lives, particularly through media. It is possible to progress towards the following goals by utilizing *Social Play*. These goals are essential to improving the educational climate of school:

1) To allow children to experience child-appropriate happiness through fun activities in school.

2) To facilitate children's attainment of higher levels of positive social interactions.

3) To stimulate children with creative and spontaneous experiences which heighten their self-expressiveness.

4) To help shape the school environment so that students receive, in an orderly and constructive fashion, positive and supportive attention, from peers and adults.

5) To provide here-and-now wholesome interactions regardless of the existing problems in a child's life whether it is poor parenting, poverty, impoverished neighborhood environment, etc.

6) To help tip the balance of student experiences to the side of cultural, creative, expressive and cooperative involvement and away from passive, violent, and bigoted ones.

7) To teach students self organization skills so they can orderly move from place to place with a minimum of direction and disorder.

Chapter 2
WHY *SOCIAL PLAY?*

Children's Developmental Needs

It is disturbing to realize the negative impact mass culture has on children. Commercial interests largely determine the content of mass culture and shape the values and habits of students in ways counter to their educational interests. Strong emphasis is placed on consumer goods via radio and television advertising and the commercialization of cultural holidays. These efforts are aimed at children.

Toys have become mass-produced, slick plastic copies of TV characters. Fewer and fewer children have the experience of making their own toys (kites, tops, scooters, models, etc.). Constructing and playing with meaningful toys is a valuable vehicle for the learning of manual skills, patience, and good self-esteem. All of these experiences and skills support classroom performance.

Another cultural pressure on children is destructive competition. The popular view of competition supports destroying one's opponent and rewards only those who win. These ideas are strongly propagated through professional, college and school sports. Why have humans developed games where there are losers? A foot race of a hundred runners will produce *ninety-nine* losers! Could this be the goal intended? No, it isn't. The reason behind competitive games is to mobilize *all* players. It is the most amazing hormonal psychological transformation of the human body, where chemicals are produced that makes one *feel as good as a human can feel.* Endorphins, acetylcholine and cortisone type hormones surge through a body when competing against a worthy opponent; pain disappears, mood is elevated and team camaraderie takes hold. *Social Play* uses competition to get children to cooperate and have fun.

A student cannot learn to think or to use deduction, logic and critical analysis, when taught racial hatred, chauvinism and intolerance. To grow up with optimum knowledge and intellect, children must be free from self destructive and self-limiting ideas. They must not, above all, be taught any kind of hatred because they will take it out on one another.

Young children must have the following developmental needs met in order to grow into well behaved students with a healthy mental attitude, and the capability and readiness to learn:

1) Need to Grow Up in a Stable Family and Community

The chances of a child having this need met are lessening with time. Changes in family structure, deteriorating urban centers, and economic demands on parents cause conditions of instability for millions of children. Add to this the pervasive fear and uncertainty caused by the threat of war, or an imminent pollution catastrophe, it is easy to see why children become psychologically and spiritually insecure about their safety and future.

Children whose parents die or abandon them are forever effected by the loss. Children raised in foster homes or by grandparents or other relatives usually long for social stability by wishing to have the "ideal" family of "mommy and daddy" restored.

The extent of this need for stability can be appreciated by examining the role that the stepmother plays in real life and in fairy tales. The fairy tale stepmother is always portrayed as "wicked" or "evil." In real life, children feel and express negative attitudes regarding stepmothers. Even if a stepmother's objective qualities are exemplary, the stepchild will usually treat that person with distrust and rejection (the older the stepchild the more likely the rejection). The reason for this seemingly irrational universal attitude towards stepmothers is that she represents what children fear the most—*instability*. It is too late for her to be accepted as an individual judged on her unique qualities because her arrival signals the loss of what the child fundamentally and desperately craves—the original, intact family.

Children's reactions to this need are played out in the classroom too. Whenever a substitute teacher enters the room, students act out against her because they are upset and angry about the instability caused by their teacher "abandoning them."

2) Need to Participate in Imagery Building Activities

This need is vital if young children are to develop abstract learning potential. Children must spend significant periods of time listening to stories read to them (fairy tales, fables and myths are best) or stories told to them by adults (especially by grandparents), and role playing activities alone or with peers (playing house, doctor and school). These imagery forming activities must be preserved or non-imaginative activities will replace them. Television viewing precludes the use of the imagination because it is a concrete stimulus preventing the viewer from forming her own mental pictures. Some research shows a correlation between early active imaginative play and a later ability to learn abstract concepts. A decrease in the use of the imagination during preschool years, can mean a decrease in the ability to grasp mathematics later on in school.

Television viewing by children as it exists today, often without limits on the amount watched, poses a threat to children's intellectual and cognitive development. SAT scores will continue to decline if physically passive, visually stimulating activities remain the dominate form of leisure activity for children.

3) Need to have Correct Balance Between Right Brain (Nonverbal, Creative and Motor Coordinated) and Left Brain (Verbal, Rational and Linear) Stimulation

The younger the child the more dominate the right brain is over the less developed left brain. As an infant ages, his language and cognitive ability improves as he develops toward a more balanced use of his right and left differential brain functions. Sometime between ten and fifteen years old, a person becomes equally proficient in right and left brain functioning. This means that younger students who are naturally right brained, cannot be expected to spend long periods trying to sit still and perform adult-type tasks. School curricula should conform more accurately to the way children function and learn.

Care should also be taken not to underestimate the perceptual and intuitive abilities of young children. Because they cannot express a concept verbally does not mean they cannot understand it. Children are generally more perceptive than adults in detecting subtle communications between people. For instance, children know when adults don't want to be with them (passive rejection) even if that desire is not openly stated. In such cases children will behave as if they are being rejected while adults will deny this (because they did not *say* it) and criticize the reaction. Verbal honesty is the best strategy in relating to children because they will perceive non-verbally what is going on.

4) Need to Play and have Fun, Free from Destructive Competition

This need has many facets. First, children must experience periods of happiness, regardless of the general condition of their lives. Second, activities must be available that are in their best interests, not in the interests of adults (parents, teachers or sports' coaches). Presently many children are being exploited by parents through sports and entertainment. Because of inadequacies in their own childhood, many parents seek their dreams vicariously through their children. They end up pushing their children to develop adult behaviors prematurely and, at the same time, deny them appropriate childhood experiences. In a magazine interview a tennis player known for his childhood successes and his adult failures said that his father pushed him into competitive tennis. "I often felt that the kind of person I was depended on how well I played and that really hurt," the player reported. Children need to know that they are valued for being themselves and not for what they produce. What purpose do report cards serve *before* middle school!

In contrast, there are constructive social activities that teach joy, kindness, friendliness, and caring for others. Children must be exposed to these activities, especially those that do not discriminate against either sex. Children's activities should also contain folklore which is an appropriate way for them to learn and understand complex social and moral values. Current television programming which is saturated with commercial, unrealistic, simple minded and violent content, perverts children and renders millions of them unable to tolerate more developmentally sound activities.

5) To be Involved in Cooperative Peer Relationships

The most obvious feature of this need is that children who learn to cooperate with peers facilitate the smooth and orderly operation of the groups in which they are members. But less obvious is the possibility that learning is a social phenomenon, not as individually motivated as many educators and parents believe. This calls for adjusting the learning environment to a more cooperative one that will support each individual in learning.

The ideal class is organized on a high social level where every child is encouraged, *by his peers*, to concentrate on learning to his potential. This is not the same as an adult saying, "Johnny can do much better work if he puts his mind to it." The reality in many schools, however, is that students are ostracized by the peer group if they are "too" studious. Peer pressure strongly attacks academic excellence and supports television watching, hanging out, drinking, smoking, and taking drugs. Even in schools with traditions of high academic achievements, the absence of a cooperative, social environment results in fiercely competitive relationships and often leads to academic dishonesty.

6) Need for Culture-Wide Rites of Passage

Presently, the growing up process is helter-skelter. Neither children or adults know of a defined or universal way of passing from childhood into adulthood. Some children run away or are kicked out of their homes when barely through puberty, while others live with parents past graduate school or longer. Some parents never wean their children, resulting in the raising of overly dependent sons and daughters, which in extreme cases, causes offspring to become disturbed and nonproductive citizens.

Children have a need to be treated in increasingly independent ways as they mature. Responsibilities and expectations should increase at a pace specific to the stage of development resulting in correctly behaving young adults. This process should be ceremonial and highly valued by the community. The Bar and Bat Mitzvah of the Jewish faith are examples of this process only it has become only symbolic (children no longer become men and women at thirteen in today's society).

A cursory study of older, non-technological societies (read Alex Haley's *Roots* for a description of a rites of passage practice) can illustrate the central role rites of passage play in advancing youth towards productive adult lives. When this process fails to operate, society suffers. Large numbers of neglected youth retaliate against the existing social order with antisocial, destructive acts. Many youth develop life styles that do not contribute to society and these examples are unjustly used to characterize all youth as "a lost generation."

It should be understood that economic opportunity is an indispensable part of the rites of passage process. Every young person must know that they will have a chance to gainfully use their education and training when they achieve adulthood. Unemployment cannot be the reward waiting at the conclusion of schooling. When this is the case, there should be no surprise that public schools attain poor results. Students have a natural reaction to this lack of opportunity—they fail to learn—what's the use!

Children's Social Needs

The most realistic way to view children's behavior is to see it as both a reaction to how they are treated by adults, and as a reflection of the extent to which their needs are met. Looking at children this way helps us to better understand the forces that shape their behavior. It also helps teachers change negative attitudes towards children, and in turn, ameliorates children's reactive behavior. When attempting to satisfy children's needs through the play experience, we also learn more accurately what needs to furnish. The understanding of the dynamics of childhood behavior can relieve many of the problems arising between children and adults, especially between teachers and students. Coupled with *Social Play* practice, this new understanding can result in exciting changes in faculty-student relationships, and can form the basis for a cooperative and viable educational environment.

In schools as in families, the social needs of children are routinely overlooked and ignored. In addition, the general culture places more and more barriers between children and the satisfaction of their needs. As a result, tension increases in the classroom. Children find fewer avenues for satisfying their needs positively, and resort to "acting out" behaviors in an attempt to meet them. We must remember that a need is something that cannot be denied, suppressed, or eliminated without causing aberrant behavior. In the classroom, children become competitors with their peers for whatever attention the teacher gives. Unfortunately, they eventually learn that disrupting the class gains them the most attention while "being good" earns less.

Knowledge of children's social needs is helpful in better understanding *Social Play*. This knowledge can assist school personnel in analyzing the effectiveness of their overall educational program as it relates to the satisfaction or violation of the social needs of its student body. When assessing social needs it is important to realize that it is the individual child who determines the amount of attention required. Some individuals are satisfied when given a little, others crave large amounts.

The following eight social needs were gleaned and distilled by the author in leading *Social Play* sessions with thousands of children.

1) Need for Social Order and Safety

The child has to feel safe enough to risk interacting with others in the environment. If he knows the rules, believes they are fair and evenly applied, he can express himself calmly.

Adults are responsible for maintaining the conditions necessary to meet this need. A well run, organized classroom provides the stable conditions required to meet this need. The responsibility is directly on the shoulders of the teacher to be a dependable leader and organizer who maintains a consistent program which provides the stability that many students lack in their own homes.

2) Need to be the Focus of Positive Attention

This need is in crisis in U.S. culture today. Attention is poorly understood, unevenly distributed and often denied those who need it most. Sports figures and movie stars are overindulged, while kids in poor neighborhoods starve.

People, and especially children, will do anything to get attention. Unfortunately, most of the time the attention elicited is negative—"Johnny, shut up or I'll send you to the Principal's office!" But the drive for meeting this need is so strong that children will continue to absorb the negative when that is all they can get. The only way to break this pattern is to structure activities to furnish group members with ample opportunities to obtain positive attention in an orderly fashion. When activities are structured this way, students begin to trust that they will receive positive attention and disruptive acts will diminish.

It must be understood that children *do not seek negative attention*. But if negative is the only kind they receive, the social order of the classroom will deteriorate into a vicious cycle where negative responses feed negative attention getting.

Another significant factor in understanding this need for attention is that it must come from the group. Many teachers confuse the individual attention that they give with social attention. If a child is receiving attention from the teacher but not from peers, little positive change will take place and the child could be further ostracized ("teacher's pet").

3) Need to have Child Appropriate Outlets for Feelings of Frustration, Aggression, and Anger

Most adults expect children to be pleasant and "good" no matter how disconcerting the environment, how neglected their needs, or how poor the role model. Nonetheless, children have many reasons to feel frustrated and angry. Conditions that cause these feelings are—incest, child abuse, racism, divorce, school problems, environmental pollution, wanton violence, poverty and unemployment (and each child has his own set of personal circumstances that are upsetting only to him). Children are virtually powerless to change society in their behalf and this renders them totally at the mercy of adults. The odds that a child will be treated well while growing up are getting slimmer in contemporary U.S. society (witness the child abuse and family violence phenomena). This is why children are angry. But generally adults deny the plight of children and do not comprehend that they are angry. Furthermore, adults are not that careful about expressing their own anger and often display inappropriate models of behavior. A prime example is the sports coach seen on TV cursing at officials and throwing a tantrum. What is appropriate and necessary is the provision of opportunities for young people to express the frustration, dislikes and anger they feel about detrimental circumstances in their lives.

The human feeling of anger has some unique and amazing qualities, some of them harmful, some of them beneficial. The potentially harmful qualities are: 1) It is non-directional, meaning that feelings of anger can be focused on anyone not just the persons or situations causing it; 2) It is accumulative and acts like electrical charges where anger producing incidences add up to a generalized feeling of anger waiting for any incidence to discharge it; 3) It can be denied, suppressed and internalized, a condition which causes somatic ills like headaches, colitis, ulcers, hypertension, depression, or stimulate alcohol and drug abuse; and 4) Anger can be expressed anti-socially either actively or passively. The active form can be verbal or physical (swearing, fighting or vandalism) while the passive aggressive form can take shape as vicious gossip or lying.

Helpful qualities of the feelings of anger are: 1) Because it is non-directional, anger can be resolved by means other than direct confrontation, such as talking with friends, parents or professionals; 2) Physiological harm can be reduced through physical activity such as exercise, sports or dramatic expression; and 3) Resolution of anger is not time limited, and positive resolution can be attained in the present of past problems.

There are some precautions to note when dealing with children and issues of anger. The major concern is avoiding reliance on verbalization. There are several reasons for this concern. One being that the younger the child, the less able he is to express ambivalent, disturbing or complex emotional issues through code words (for instance, divorce). Secondly, discussing anger can result in amplifying the intensity of the feelings instead of resolving them. And finally, talking is the least efficient form of anger resolution due to the flight/fight design of Homo Sapiens. In humans, anger has hormonal body chemistry components which require *physical activity* for dissipation. Running, chasing, tagging, laughing (playing) does it while sitting, and talking (passivity) does not.

The author has rediscovered what he considers to be a forgotten social law. It is: *The optimum resolution of anger takes place in the social realm, not in the individual, one-to-one mode, and that cultural, social activities (play, dance and drama) are the most effective forms of controlling anger in humans.* During the *Social Play* experience players forgive and forget those who made them angry in previous encounters, and they discover and establish the more pleasurable aspects of a relationship. This discovery, a major reason for offering this book, is a useful and powerful tool which resolves anger in a harmless manner. When group members are not combative, tremendous amounts of friendly human energy is released, and this energy can be used to help a group accomplish its tasks. The classroom is where this process reaps the most benefits.

4) Need for Integrated Functions

This need becomes more important as society becomes more technological. Tasks are so specialized that it is easy to overlook that children are *whole beings* and need to be involved simultaneously in the intellectual, the affective, and the motor realms. In education, this need is often overshadowed because teachers feel responsible for educating children mainly in the cognitive domain to prepare them for success in a commercial, technological, work environment which eliminates, for the most part, a physical component. To function well as a specialist for large periods of time, individuals must spend commensurate amounts of time in integrating cultural activities which bring contentment to their existence.

While in school, children are asked to separate into functioning areas that are difficult for them, that is, spending large periods of time being physically inactive and cognitively involved. The younger the children the harder it is for them to remain in this state, because younger children depend so heavily on the psychomotor and affective areas of functioning. Their cognitive abilities become more operative as they mature. With this model in mind, one can see how activities which restrict children's natural balance of integrated functioning, and requires them to suppress ways of functioning that are more useful to them, can cause stress and discomfort. It is surely the goal of education to guide children to a mature level of cognitive functioning and be able to sustain long periods of nonintegrated functioning. But requiring this mature mode of behavior prematurely, is unrealistic and counterproductive.

The best learning environment includes not only the activities that contain all the elements of children's functioning areas but also in the proportions that are matched to each child's maturity level with enough leeway for growth. The youngest students need many more affective and physical forms, while the older student is capable of handling more cognitive ones. When successfully involved in integrated functioning a child will recall that experience as a "good time" or "fun." When forced to suppress areas of functioning, children will either forget or loathe the experience. Lack of integrated functioning in the school experience is frequently responsible for anxiety among students (and is responsible for the "I hope the school burns down!" student wish). The opposite reaction, a relaxed and happy feeling, results from a program rich in integrating activities.

5) Need for Intimate Proximity

Children need to be touched, stroked, and tickled well past the preschool years. Touching remains a need because of the intense, fundamental role nurturing plays in the development of the human infant. During the school years this need widens to include the intimate proximity of peers. Children who do not receive a minimum amount of touching can become tactile defensive, withdrawn, and suspicious— unable to develop fully intimate human interactions. The educational function of schools is best served when children tolerate normal touching without responding with hostile retaliation or escalating into physical conflict.

A serious barrier to meeting this need concerns the erroneous view that equates general intimate proximity with sexual proximity. This can be readily observed starting around third grade. During fourth and fifth grades a simple hand holding activity will elicit gross sexual rejection based on boys and girls refusing to touch one another, and in high school, boys will suffer extreme censure from peers eluding to homosexuality if normal touch takes place outside rough, "manly" activities. These practices limit the healthy interactions between students. Normal touch needs are blocked out and sex is prematurely injected into relationships that in no way should be considered sexual.

When school programs fail to help children develop healthy attitudes and relationships between peers, male and female, learning is seriously curtailed because useful activities cannot be conducted and too much energy is used in fighting, rejecting and withdrawing from peers.

6) Need to Experience Self and Others Non-Critically

Our culture is governed by aggressive and competitive forces, and life has become fast paced and materially oriented. Strong critical pressures arise in this life-style and mold interpersonal relationships. It becomes nearly impossible to avoid being seen for shortcomings, and people are viewed that way in their jobs, marriages and schools. It is in education that this overly critical way of relating goes to the extreme—failures are published and made permanent via the report card!

Most children do not hold up well under constant negative scrutiny. They handle it by giving it right back. Life then becomes a series of "dog-eat-dog" struggles in which they use their energy defending themselves and attacking others. This form of interaction seriously detracts from students learning in school. Spending a little time in a average middle school will bear witness to this statement. This flaw in our way of life seriously affects children.

7) Need to Feel Ethnic Pride and Tolerance Towards Others

The single greatest failure of U.S. democracy has been the failure of its leadership to resolve issues of bigotry, prejudice and racism. From slave times to the present, bigotry and racism have played a part in American life, despite the pronouncements that America is a democracy and a melting pot. This flaw in our way of life seriously affects children.

Children, especially when young, are completely and naturally oblivious to seeing and judging people as "different" because of skin color. But they eventually succumb to it if constantly exposed to it. Being forced to adopt racist beliefs upset children's orientation to the natural world, and diminishes their humanity when they are cultivated into its practice. Those who are made to believe in intolerance and racial hatred become vulnerable to the same practices. There is no defense against bigotry once racism against others is accepted. *A child taught prejudice is also its victim.* They are denied the ability and the right to form beneficial relationships or reject harmful ones.

Surprisingly, the most widespread form of intolerance in schools is not racial—it is sexual. It is seen as the "girls versus the boys" syndrome. In many communities, boys openly express male chauvinistic attitudes in the presence of girls (racist ideology is generally not expressed so openly). Many teachers and Principals accept as "natural" or "cute" this battle between the sexes. Others think it not necessarily positive but just a "passing phase" appearing around fourth grade and disappearing later on. These views are inaccurate; the "battle of the sexes" continues to seriously affect relationships between men and women all life long. Close observation will show that schools contribute to developing these harmful attitudes between boys and girls by failing to include activities and organizational forms that prevent these chauvinist attitudes from flourishing. Schools are full of sexually stereotyping practices. Including sexually segregated schools, separate gym programs, teacher attitudes like, "Girls, would you get Mr. Aycox some punch, and I need four strong boys to move the tables." or "Girls, lineup, now boys, line up." Text books contain sexist material like photos showing boys being active and girls holding their hands in their laps, etc., etc. etc.

All forms of intolerance towards human beings is socially destructive to children. It inhibits meeting social needs, and they preclude having the activities that benefit students in learning about and appreciating each other. In a multinational, "democratic" society, learning to understand and appreciate others is a vital prerequisite for having successful schools.

8) Need to Express Positively the Uniqueness of One's Personality in the Social Sphere Without Being "put down"

This need is simply feeling safe enough to sing without a good voice, to act without star credits, and to be spokesperson for oneself without being ignored. In social groups, the need exists for all members to be equals as human beings, to be valued for their unique personalities and not always for their performance.

When this need is met, hostile name calling will diminish among children. This would be a giant step in humanizing school relationships, especially if children stopped calling others "retards."

Self-Esteem at School

The eighties and nineties saw an intense surge of interest in student self-esteem. At best, most of these programs did not go to the root of the problem and at worst many were patronizing (telling children their work is good when it is not). First of all, school is not the main place where students experience good feelings about themselves. School is a critical, judgmental institution. This is the nature of testing and grading. If students have difficulty with school subjects or with their behavior, they will suffer a lowering of self-esteem. In addition, teachers, either consciously or subconsciously, prefer smart, well-behaved students—they do not like poor performing, misbehaving ones.

In this environment, where does the average or poor student find encouragement? As schools are presently organized only the exceptional scholar or athlete derives pride from school. If not at school, where does a child go to find self-esteem?

Childhood self-esteem comes mainly from having an active play life! Play provides activities for children to learn and gain competency—*without being judged and rated by adults.* The play has to be diverse so each child can find the things in which they can excel. It it's not baseball, it may be kickball. If it is not jump rope, it may be jacks. If none of these, maybe it is drawing. Compulsory school subjects are *adult* selected activities neither natural nor suited for every child. The skills acquired through play are what gives children high self-esteem. These feelings of competency are what allows them to tolerate and succeed at classroom learning.

Another factor in children feeling good is being physically active. Without adequate amounts of aerobic and muscular activity, children do not produce the brain chemistry for elevated moods. Involvement in *Social Play* primarily teaches children social skills. Though not generally as vigorous as sports, playing social games provides lots of movement. In so many schools today, there is very little time in the schedule for recess or gym. Imagine yourself a child again and made to stay in a room for over *five hours without adequate* physical activity! Children grow developmentally sound if they are active—not when passively watching others do.

For schools to be more helpful in this area, they must broaden their activity base. This is especially true when urban street play is precarious because of safety issues and suburb playmates are too far away. In school the amount of physical play activity must increase because the amount of passivity in the rest of a child's life has increased over the years.

Cooperative Learning

Cooperative learning is also becoming more popular in schools. It is high time this idea has come to the classroom. In industry, everyone must cooperate and share knowledge if the work effort is to bear fruit. Can you imagine a business meeting where everyone does his own work and refuses to present their findings to co-workers! This is precisely how schools have taught students for generations. Now it's time to realize what a handicap this is in a modern, interdependent, technological world.

However, many teachers are having trouble making the cooperative method work. Why? Because parents want *their* child to do better at school than their neighbor's child. Why? Because of college acceptance, financial aid and scholarships. So many teachers get plenty of resistance. Students complain about who is assigned to their work group and often refuse to share in the group effort. They also criticize and belittle their teammates.

Social Play is the best way to prepare students to accept cooperative learning initiatives. It effectively teaches the values of cooperating and sharing.

Chapter 3
MAKING THE SYSTEM WORK

Leadership Philosophy

Social Play leadership philosophy rests firmly on the belief that positive and capable leadership is vital to all stable groups. Good *Social Play* practice places the burden of group outcome on the leadership. How the leader listens to and responds to group members determines the well-being and success of the group. If a leader considers group members antagonists, leads them demagogically, or fails to protect them from avoidable harm, the group process will be problematical.

Social Play leadership, as it influences the group process, consists of two components: philosophy (ideology and values); and technique (skills in communication and persuasion). Good technique without purposeful intent is not sufficient to accomplish goals nor does strong ideology coupled with weak practice accomplish anything but disorder, frustration and disappointment. Children despise poor leadership—either dictatorial and punitive or weak and vacillating. Both styles of leadership are unworthy of children's respect.

Leadership Techniques

Games leadership technique seems simple but its influence on *Social Play* outcomes should not be underestimated. Cultivating good technique requires practicing until an effective style is mastered. If a leader's technique is slipshod, the *Social Play* sessions may actually add to existing problems instead of alleviating them. However, when leadership technique is polished, the educator can set into motion the play dynamics that bring about positive social change. In addition, the educator will gain insights into how children learn to change negative behaviors into positive ones.

While involved in game playing, both leader and players will notice some individuals display new, more suitable behaviors. Group members, including the leader, will reinforce these behaviors and expect them to carry over into other activities. This is the theory of expectations which is widely held regarding cognitive performance. Simply stated, it says that if a teacher is told (erroneously) and believes a student to be either gifted or limited, the student's achievements will be in accordance with the teacher's expectations and not with the student's real ability. In *Social Play*, the powerful effects of expectation is all the more powerful because *all* members of the group, not just the teacher, will expect better behavior from those individuals who need to improve their social functioning.

The Techniques

1) Use the organizational command! The group must be in formation before giving rules. Give organizational commands, that is, "Everyone move your chairs back and come stand in a circle!" This type direction is magical—it is always obeyed, especially if you convey it in a firm and friendly manner (it's a projection that you know what you are doing). Learn to randomly divide a group into teams quickly, without losing control or causing confusion. *This technique is the key to leading successful Social Play sessions.*

2) Know the games. Don't be fooled by their apparent simplicity. It is important to know every rule and detail of a game, otherwise there may be confusion and disorder. A game failure is to be avoided at all costs! Make sure you know the number of chairs needed.

3) Move furniture to make play space, and enlist the help of group members to do so. This lets the group know you have the authority to structure the environment so they can have fun. It is also a good use of anxious pre-play energy.

4) Start enthusiastically and positively. Don't ask meekly if the group wants to play, for they may say, "We don't want to play any silly games!" This is less likely to happen with younger children, but is a real possibility when dealing with junior and senior high students.

5) Have equipment ready. Don't delay play by wandering off to find an empty waste basket or a blindfold; the group may get out of control while you are gone. Don't trust phonographs, CD players or tape players. Test them before you plan music games and always have a spare player handy when playing away from the classroom.

6) Make instructions brief and get the game started quickly. Explain additional rules later if they are not necessary at the beginning. Don't let questioners derail getting started; cut off endless questioning by saying, "Let's play!" Most questions will clear up then.

7) Always run a demonstration round before officially starting. The rule of thumb is to talk less and demonstrate more. A few students will learn from your words alone, most will learn from a combination of words and action, and the few remaining students will catch on after play has lasted a few rounds. Make it clear that the demonstration will not count.

8) Project your presence and voice to enable all to see and hear you. Rotate and repeat rules when talking in a circle. Encourage all players to talk up so everyone can hear them too. Bring large groups in close (keeping them in playing formation) while explaining the rules, then move them back to their playing positions after the rules are stated.

9) Do not tell the players *how* to play the game—just establish the rules. If you violate this technique, you will be depriving the players of the reasons for playing the games—individual discovery and problem solving. You do not want to be the coach, you want your players to interpret on their own. Problem solving is what makes social games a valuable experience. When players find themselves in a novel situation and figure out a solution, this is the moment of fun, self-esteem and growth!

10) Discipline positively. Point out contrary behavior as the game is being played, but try not to disrupt play to do it. If many students are acting negatively, ask yourself whether it is the right game to play with the group. If not, change the game to one that the group can handle. It is a wise *Social Play* leader that will involve the entire group in helping to censure deviant behavior of individuals and avoid personal, one-on-one struggles. Say, "Do others feel that Johnny's ruining the game?"

11) End a game near or at its high point. This is easier said than done. Practice and experiment to help improve this aspect of your leadership technique. If a game is allowed to last too long it becomes boring and players will show this by yawning, proposing changes in the rules, suggesting another game or asking to go to the bathroom. If cut off too soon—before some players have understood the game or not enough players are involved—the game will not make an impact on the players. If a game is stopped at its peak, students will beg to continue and will request playing the game again. If a game has scoring, the winning tally should be set after several rounds have been played. This will allow you to best determine a winning score which will end the game near its peak of enjoyment.

12) Become a player after the game is taught and running smoothly, but *never relinquish control*. Re-exert yourself as leader if a problem arises. Do not hesitate to step in and stop play if overly negative events take place. Either restore the play or initiate a discussion of the incident that disrupted it. The players will astound you with their honesty concerning the behavior that caused the need for discussion. This happens in part because the students love playing the games and are highly motivated to monitor misbehaving so as not to jeopardize having fun.

13) Do not give in to requests to play a favorite game over and over (you wear out a game by playing it too frequently). Play a different game instead.

14) Sharpen your expertise and broaden your repertoire. This will enable you to best meet the class's needs, instead of trying to fit their needs into your limited range. The best way to learn a game is to first experience it as a player, then lead it among peers, and finally offer it to your students.

Chapter 4
BEHAVIOR PROBLEMS IN THE SCHOOLS

Ten Classroom Problems and *Social Play* Remedies

Due mainly to a lack of a psycho dynamic understanding of human social needs and behavior, teaching has become a bewildering and stressful profession. Teachers who receive training that view school children as individuals fall victim to ineffective practices in dealing with their students. This happens because students, in the classroom, are not individuals—they are *peer group social beings.* At times, entire faculties unknowingly accept negative and nonsocial attitudes towards their students. This results in frustrating and counterproductive classroom management strategies. These strategies fail because they are not based on the actual reasons students behave the way they do. Presented here are ten such school problems along with possible *Social Play* solutions.

1) Acceptance of Low Expectations of Students

This belief holds that children have limited abilities (based on "intelligence" tests, student wealth, appearance, or minority status) instead of recognizing and dealing with problems that hamper their potential.

Social Play experience expands the range of expression available to a student. It does this by not only demanding *from* him but also *rewards* him (meets his social needs). Human beings cannot be expected to give up behaviors that are not acceptable to others simply because they are asked to do so. Every person has reasons for their actions and must be given useful alternatives in order to change. *Social Play* simultaneously integrates a child's emotional and physical self. Students having difficulty with any single area of functioning become uncomfortable and unresponsive when restricted to that mode of functioning. But students can improve in areas of weakness when they are able to rely on other strengths. In this way they will experience improvement instead of failure, thereby boosting self confidence. This is exactly the kind of experiential structure that social games provide.

Students can also be encouraged to higher levels of performance if their peer group is supportive. This form of encouragement is far more effective than teachers and parents pressuring students with the old familiar, "Johnny, we know you can do better." For peer encouragement to come about, teachers must be skilled in organizing their classrooms into cooperative and cohesive communities. These kinds of student groups can be eager about learning. *Social Play* is indispensable in assisting when teachers pursue this goal.

2)   Preoccupation with Students' Failures

When material is presented to a child and the child cannot process it, a failing grade is given (and made permanent via the report card). If students don't learn by making mistakes, how do they learn? Why is failure seen as more important than discovery? After a few years of absorbing this treatment, students become preoccupied with their own shortcomings, and fear failure instead of enjoying learning. An example will explain. When leading a geography game in a classroom the class was divided into competing groups. The groups were instructed to name, without use of maps or books, as many countries as they could beginning with the letter C. The team with the greatest number of correct countries would be the winner. After the session, one student came to the leader and sadly said, "Our team didn't do too well." The leader excitedly answered, "Your team did the best!" "But we lost. We had fewer correct answers," she insisted. "But that's just it," replied the leader, "You learned the most!" She looked perplexed for a moment as she tried to understand this positive statement. "I guess you're right," she said brightening just a little as she still struggled with the concept.

In *Social Play,* students are rewarded for problem-solving—figuring out what is wrong and correcting it. In addition, they are often given the power to control the group, thus receiving positive attention even if they "mess up." In *Social Play,* students are not condemned by a permanent record if their behavior is ignorant or antisocial; students are supported in their efforts to improve.

3)   Schools Must Punish the Disruptive Student

Most often the punishment for the disruptive child is isolation from their class. The student is ordered out of the classroom, is sent to the principal or is suspended. This approach is justified, not because it is effective in changing the student's behavior, but because it will bring relief and reestablish order. Isolation is a poor method of disciplining students because it is punitive and illogical. Did the misbehaving child transgress solely against the teacher? Disruptive students disrupt entire classes, not just the teacher (authority). This raises the question of who should be concerned? The entire class should be involved in managing behaviors that disrupt it. When the teacher deals with the "problem child" alone, a one-on-one struggle ensures. The odds that a teacher can win these struggles are slim and what is more, she can lose control of the class, too. Teacher arbitrariness and anger enters into the struggle and the student vents hostility on the teacher and the clash escalates and deepens. *The disruptive student ends up getting more attention than well behaved students!* Other students observe this and conclude that disruption gains more of the teacher's attention than being well behaved. The classroom social order is put in jeopardy when this chain of events takes place.

When insufficient understanding exists regarding the motives underlying the disruptive incidents, there can be no resolution of the problem. Temporary isolation of a student is a makeshift solution, and eventually the cycle of misbehaving and punishment returns. The student's behavior is a signal that something is wrong but this issue is seldomly addressed.

Social Play addresses this problem in several ways. First, "acting-out" classroom behaviors diminish when *Social Play* is incorporated into the curriculum because attention is made available to attention starved students through the play. Second, *Social Play* provides the teacher with a format for shaping the class into a more cohesive community. Social problems can be positively resolved in a community through sharing the opinions of all group members in consideration of the behavior of the disruptive student. Respected opinions are expressed by classmates along with feelings of concern for the "problem child" and personal struggling with the teacher is minimized. *The censure of antisocial behavior by an entire group is the only reality that disruptive students heed in a non-combative way.*

4) Teachers Become Caught up in Personality Clashes with Students

Personality clashes between teacher and the "pain in the neck" student occur for reasons which escape most teachers. The classic reason is the vying of *two* leaders for control. Children have leadership qualities and abilities, but traditional thought leads teachers to believe that they are the *only* capable leaders in the classroom. This is not true. Many students are exceedingly perceptive and capable of spotting weaknesses in their teacher's leadership ability. These students tend to make critical remarks or disrupt the class. If the teacher fails to understand the true nature of the conflict, she will fall into an on-going struggle with that child. The solution to the problem is achieved when the student is given a legitimate and appropriate leadership role in the class structure which is under the teacher's overall leadership.

Initial *Social Play* sessions provide the information needed to ascertain which students have leadership potential. Subsequent sessions will provide students with opportunities to experience the leadership role in various games. Any leadership needs not met in the games would have to be addressed through assignments in other classroom roles.

5) Students are not Expected to Know Their Classmates Well

Students are involved in years of schooling with a surprising result—they do not get to know one another. Students sit in the same classroom from September until June but are not comfortable in the class, because they don't really know that much about their classmates (see children's letters in the Appendix). How can this be, when so much time is spent together in the classroom? This phenomenon exists because sensitivity to this issue is rare, it's seen as unimportant, and teachers fail to involve students in activities which facilitate their getting to know one another. The significance of this issue is more pronounced when changes take place in the classroom composition. For example, when a new student is added during the semester, unless time is spent integrating the new personality into the group, tremendously upsetting changes can take place. The new child can feel shut out while the original class members can resent his arrival and the adjustments forced on the class. *Social Play* is the ideal medium for solving these critical issues in the social group process. Allowing group members to become increasingly familiar and friendly is a natural outcome of *Social Play*.

6)   Students' Physical/Motor Needs are Neither Addressed nor Understood

An example of the lack of attention paid to the physical area is the expectation that a child should stay orderly and quiet for the entire school day. Another problem is holding infrequent physical education classes. Why is this physical need important in school? What is the relationship between intellectual and motor functioning? In children this relationship is strong. The meeting of physical/motor needs assists students to function successfully in more passive, cognitive tasks. Physical activity has the physiological effect of calming the nervous system and alerting the intellect.

Most schools have a recess period, but a popular misconception about its use still persists. Many teachers believe that you have to "tire'em out" before they will settle down. This is an incomplete oversimplification of the hormonal dynamics of a child's active to passive behavioral mechanisms. It is true that physical activity produces brain stimulating hormones (acetylcholine, adrenaline and endorphins) necessary for learning to take place, but expending energy is not the single factor in helping students cope with self-control. The context and quality of the use of energy is crucial. Socially directed, organized activity helps students learn and develop all phases of behavior. In most recess periods, however, students run amuck, fight and disrupt. They exhibit misdirected play, habits like throwing balls at those not playing, and impoverished play, which is excessive arguing and fighting while playing. This kind of disordered, chaotic experience never calms students. In fact, many of the fights and conflicts originating in such recess periods carry over into the classroom and wind up in the principal's office.

When active play is socially organized it helps students deal with their emotions and energy-use constructively. However, this occurs only when the play environment is structured positively. As a result, appropriate outlets and interactions take place and negative behaviors subside. The students learn to have their physical needs met and to play in more socially acceptable and beneficial ways. Eventually peers will monitor their own play during recess with out needing adults to keep order. When this pattern is established, each successive class learns how to play socially helpful games from the preceding one.

When school personnel learn *Social Play* games and implement them at recess time (especially useful during indoor recess) the students learn to become more socially organized during these periods. Subsequently, teachers shed their dread of recess duty and often enjoy playing too. As a result, everyone develops more tolerant opinions and feeling towards each other. An atmosphere of positive energy is created which also supports cognitive learning.

7)   Students are Made to Deal Too Often in the Past and Future Realms

Children are basically *here and now* beings. The younger the child the less able he is to process adult messages and warnings about past mistakes or future obstacles. Most of children's conscious learning is centered in the *here and now*. Most teachers and parents admonish, attempt to correct, or punish students for an incident that happened in the past ("Wait 'til your father gets home!"). This method generates fear in the child but it does not facilitate learning. The child becomes fearful and confused during the interim between the behavior and punishment. The circumstances around the behavior becomes fuzzy for the child and at the same time his anxiety level increases. It is a dilemma for the child, a confusing situation that is stressful but hardly conducive to learning.

When a child is involved in *Social Play,* moral or behavioral messages are effective (for example, not to boo or hurt others) because they are linked to the behavior at the time of the incident. Because the child is invested in the activity (having fun), where his transgression takes place, *and* the leader warns publicly that the fun is jeopardized by his behavior, the child usually internalizes quickly and changes his response. The child learns the lesson being taught through the game because it is in his *own self-interest* not the teacher's. Teachers are always amazed when they witness this *Social Play* phenomena. *Social Play* can successfully eliminate bothersome behaviors that traditional approaches fail to extinguish.

8)   Schools Lack Respect for Students (Especially in Poor Neighborhoods and in High Schools) and Students do not Learn to Respect Each Other

Many schools have an antagonistic and cynical atmosphere. They lack a spirit of curiosity, optimism and youthfulness among their student bodies and faculty. It is as though someone has told the staff that their students were incorrigible, worthless and dull, and that they should be treated harshly, spoken to condescendingly, and not to be trusted. This attitude is evident in the manner and tone of voice that the faculty speaks to their students. The students naturally try to defend themselves by making school life difficult for teachers. It becomes similar to a 'class struggle' where no one escapes the antagonisms between students and teachers, including those teachers (almost all new teachers) who have not adopted cynical and negative postures towards students.

It's difficult to discover who is responsible for initiating this struggle or when it began. The conflict is so entrenched that many think the situation is "natural" and impossible to change. But it is possible to make changes with *Social Play*. If school personnel show more respect for students, students will show more respect for each other. When high school students are convinced that faculty respect them, they respond by showing respect to teachers and to themselves.

9)   Students Fail to Learn Communication Skills

This is because teachers receive most of the focus of attention. Students learn good speaking skills only if they have ample opportunities practicing in groups. They learn to write when asked to tell about topics of interest to themselves. Students do not learn when they are constantly lectured, assigned arbitrary topics for writing assignments or subject to a classroom where the social mood is more critical than supportive. Students will not risk performing in this kind of group. The teaching style where students are called on like victims and are belittled if they do not give the right answer also suppress students from venturing to learn speaking skills. In such classrooms only the most knowledgeable and skilled member will perform and that person is the teacher!

Social Play measures out and distributes attention so all members get a chance to learn and practice speaking skills without ridicule. Writing skills develop because *Social Play* makes students feel secure in expressing their feelings. It works incredibly well!

10) Physical Education and Competition are used with the Wrong Emphasis

There are two fundamental ways to look at competition. One is the mainstream economic-political view which espouses competition as a struggle to defeat one's opponent, drive him out of business, acquire his property, or destroy him (ultimate method is war). Schools reflect this doctrine in their drive to be champions in extramural sports. *Social Play* views competition differently. It holds that competition is a significant human interaction that should be used positively and not to harm people. In social games, competition is used to mobilize players to higher levels of cooperation. This is accomplished *without* stressing winning over others. No value is placed on defeating an opponent; the opponent is there to interact with during the game and to increase the level of fun. There is no motivation to eliminate play opponents. *Social Play* sees competition as a valuable instrument in assessing student's skill levels in comparison to others and in measuring their progress in performance areas. *Social Play* rejects competitive successes or failures as a measure of one's worth.

The embracing of *Social Play* ideas and methods will raise questions about physical education as it is practiced today. Should the development of highly skilled, coached student athletes be a primary concern of physical education teachers? When this is the case, a disproportionate level of influence is exerted on the overall school program despite the fact that superior athletic development is not a fundamental educational function. In addition, this system can be corrupted and compromised by pressures from college and professional sports interests. The more successful the sports programs are, the more the masses of average students are neglected by the teaching/coaching staff. Subsequently, educational funds are used to do a first rate job for the few athletically talented athletes (mostly males) and a poor job with the majority of students. P.E. teachers often become scouts and coaches with attitudes that cause them to be insensitive teachers who relate poorly to the students who are not athletically precocious and interested in competitive sports. This situation undermines the academic integrity of schools. Recruitment abuses, falsifying of transcripts, and other scandals are widespread and frequently exposed in the press. Should school athletes have to maintain a minimum grade to be eligible for participation in sports is a controversial issue when extramural athletics are based in schools. Should academic performance be linked to athletic privilege?

A better alternative to the present system would be a program consisting of these components: an organized daily aerobic/flexibility session designed to support the academic program; a P.E. curriculum that would teach lifelong sports (non-coached) aimed at the average skill level and designed to systematically introduce every student to the rudiments of a wide range of sports (to give the broadest number of students a chance to discover some area of competency); an intramural sports program in which all student participate with their classmates, including a screening procedure to select the exceptionally coordinated student for recommendation to a sports club. These clubs would operate after school, be skill oriented and could be publicly or privately funded. The sports club would have no corrupting influence over the schools. The club would be the domain of the coach and extramural leagues; the schools would be the domain of the P.E. teacher. The P.E. teacher would be responsible for teaching *Social Play* games, folk and popular dance, fitness, health, nutrition, anatomy, non-coached sports, and do it in a wholesome manner with emphasis on involvement, fair play and fun. The home room teacher could be responsible for the daily aerobic/flexibility session.

For a Better Understanding of Student/Teacher Problems

Teachers constantly find themselves in a dilemma. They are expected to teach large numbers of students who are difficult to handle. Increasing numbers of students are undisciplined, disruptive, belligerent and suffer emotional and learning difficulties. Teachers are nevertheless expected to manage and teach these students without sufficient training or support. It is understandable that teachers wish that they had students who didn't come from troubled homes, but complaining about family life doesn't help. It makes matters worse because it focuses on the areas of their student's life outside their control. It also diverts the teacher's attention and energy away from seeking ways to deal more effectively with their students as they are, including securing the necessary supports.

Another part of the dilemma is the lack of methodology to turn the difficult-to-control students into better behaved ones. In an attempt to make positive changes in the students, some atrocious methods are used. Progressive, child-appropriate techniques are not widely understood or practiced. Adopting *Social Play* techniques can spur movement towards a healthy shift in approach. Let us examine critically some prevalent methods used in dealing with student's behavior in school.

Exhortation

"Johnny, if you don't stop calling out, I'm going to paddle you!" This threatens but doesn't change anything because it is just venting by the teacher and is not connected in any way to the reasons for the behavior. Besides, verbal instruction is not the strongest area of learning for children. Their best mode is doing through guided experience. It is not easy to stop exhorting students but realizing that it is not effective helps to lessen relying on it to change anything.

Punishment

It permeates the thinking of school personnel and all its forms are vindictive. Corporal punishment is potentially dangerous because it is primitive and can physically, if not mentally, harm children. It is difficult to control (witness child abuse) and the person administering it can become subjective and angry. Using a writing assignment (I will not do such-and-such again over and over hundreds of times) to punish is a totally counterproductive and self-defeating practice, and it should be a thing of the past. *Teachers should never use what they teach as punishment!*

Isolation

This is a great favorite as a punishment. It really is an admission that no solution to a behavior problem is known and is an attempt to make the problem disappear. But the problem always resurfaces and usually with a vengeance. Isolating students from the social group teaches the child that he is incorrigible, builds resentment in the child towards those he is forced to leave. Social isolation is a severe form of human punishment because it destroys the ability of a person to relate positively to others. It is used that way as torture in prisons. *Isolation has no positive use in institutions dealing with children.*

Detention

It is a form of punishment that backfires. If school is a good place and learning is desirable, student should naturally like school. Then the more time the student spends there, the more she benefits. How could this be punishment? Because for many students the school experience is a drudgery. *Only schools that fail to educate can use detention as punishment.*

Taken as a whole the punishment scene in schools reveal glaring failures in the socio-educational practices of educators and this can lead to recalcitrant students and police-like or burned-out teaching staffs. So far, teacher training has not derived a child-appropriate, effective method, based on a realistic understanding of childhood behavioral dynamics, to assist students in learning good behavior as well as mastering school subjects.

Nearly every disciplinary method currently in use fails to establish an activity base (*doing* is the best learning mode for children) whereby the students can have opportunities to select and experience appropriate behaviors and not merely listen to adults lecture to them what to do (the least effective mode of learning for children). Children must make mistakes to learn, but few programs allow for this. Usually, students are condemned instead of corrected.

The increasingly individualized outlook of education only serves to isolate students from their peers. Students learn best when they are knowledgeable of their classmates and receive the broadest possible support in correcting areas of weakness. This includes peers as well as teachers. Individualistic ideas and programs simply cut off these supportive contacts. What is needed is a more social-based teacher training where teachers learn how to shape classes into cohesive learning communities. When this is done, more students will learn socially acceptable behavior, a prerequisite of academic learning. This will take place despite their living in homes and communities that are less than ideal.

The Teacher and *Social Play*

It is imperative that educators understand that students' learning experiences must be balanced between competing as individuals against peers (valued for performance) and as a cooperating, supportive social being (valued as a unique personality). Teachers interested in utilizing *Social Play* must strive to learn to apply *Social Play* techniques under the latter principle and not the former. Social games can be made impotent if the leader does not understand the difference between playing to learn and feeling good about oneself and one's peers or playing to win, the symbolic destruction of one's opponent. Students new to *Social Play* quickly learn the difference and savor the experience when the leader presents the games in the correct spirit.

Constant exhorting and belittling students are negative controlling forms and cause more problems than they solve. Relating to students in this way is devoid of concrete learning activities in which the child can learn step-by-step, progressively higher levels of social behavior. Punishment and disciplinary approaches that antagonize the child and frustrate the practitioner, fuels a "them-against-us" struggle. These roles are played out in schools all over the nation. What is missing in school systems is a rudimentary understanding as how to call a truce, disengage and regroup into more pleasant, meaningful relationships.

Social Play offers an orderly process for the seemingly impossible task of improving student behaviors and establishing more youthful and smoothly run schools. The fundamental *Social Play* process is the mobilization of the peer group into a powerful force for counteracting antisocial behaviors and rewarding cooperative ones. Social group peer pressure, when guided by sound leadership and applied within an activity, is more effective in shaping positive relationships than individual authority.

The leader need only to depend on the power of authority in times when the group can't maintain itself, when social demands exceed the group's capacity, or when a particularly powerful personality overwhelms the group (this can happen frequently in classes containing troubled youth). It is important that the leader not abdicate the authority role completely, that role being indispensable to the positive outcome of the *Social Play* process and depended on by students as the anchor that stabilizes the social environment.

Teachers must overcome the fear that they will lose their authority if their students have fun with them. If *Social Play* leadership techniques are introduced and mastered, the resulting successful game playing will not only improve the teacher's authority role, but will initiate the process whereby the students will surprise and astound the teacher with new positive behaviors that disprove negative and false views of the students. These positive experiences will help the teacher gain higher levels of understanding of not only the social needs of the students but also what they need from adults as leaders. *Social Play* sessions will assist teachers in helping the student to:

1)   *Learn positive social behaviors.*

2)   *Learn to increase self control.*

3)   *Be more socially organized (fire drills will go better).*

4)   *Learn to delay gratification and control impulses.*

5)   *Learn to enjoy the **here-and-now** and feel worthy of pleasure.*

6)   *Advance communication skills both verbally and non-verbally.*

7)   *Foster a positive attitude towards writing and speaking as good ways to express feelings instead of acting out.*

8)   *Learn the value of cooperating with and supporting peers in the classroom community.*

9)   *Learn to rely on intrinsic values and not prizes.*

10)   *Increase use of mental imagery building.*

11) Learn body coordination free of stressful performance anxiety.

12) Gain experience in social problem solving.

13) Be able to modulate shifting between active and calm states.

14) Adopt a happier and more respectful view of school and eliminate name-calling, fighting and vandalism.

All students will improve in these areas, including those in every grade, ability and socioeconomic level. Exceptional students in special education programs will also benefit greatly through being involved in the therapeutic benefits of *Social Play*.

Chapter 5
THE GAMES

Play—More Than Fun

Play is a vital, indispensable *biological* activity. It is essential to the dissipation of the stresses in the adult world and is vital to the normal development of children.

Play integrates the conscious and the subconscious. It is simultaneously serious and frivolous. It restructures the environment by establishing simple yet powerful rules that change relationships and interactions into those that differ from the real, non-play world. Play forms the basis for experiencing happiness and fun. It allows the *here-and-now* to preempt the preoccupation with past regrets, or the fear of future uncertainties. During *Social Play*, creative, wholesome, social stimuli replaces negative, selfish drives.

Play is a reprieve from the seriousness of the day-to-day struggle for survival. It is a "time out" that allows relaxation, healing and renewal to take place, as well as enabling a later, stronger reentry into the harsher realities of life. Play functions like sleep; it recharges us and helps us reorganize our social outlook more positively. Play, therefore, is an invaluable human activity.

The Social Game—A Special Kind of Play

Games and play are popular concepts that are universally practiced. We play games known as sports, using bats, balls and bases. We indulge in ancient table games such as chess, backgammon and cards. We purchase millions of dollars of Chinese checkers, dominoes, word and other games. We play jacks, hop scotch and jump rope. We watch TV quiz games and spend hours playing the newest form of game, the electronic game. What has all but disappeared from our play life is *social games*.

What is a social game and why is it advocated so strongly in this book? The social game is a special form of play that gets people to relate to others. It does not require fancy equipment or emphasize winning. It uses competition to foster cooperation and allows the players to get to know one another as personalities not as adversaries. This social content is what makes these games unique. Social games are not used commercially (for profit) nor do they have leagues or professional players. They are played by groups who have an expressed need or desire to be cohesive, productive, and friendly. Social games need not be practiced or perfected since the primary skills they develop are social in nature and help people express their personalities in a positive way.

Most social games have either an *It* role or cooperative teams. The *It* is never the object of ridicule or the butt of a joke. On the contrary, the *It* is often the person who has 'messed up' but is rewarded and not reprimanded. Instead he receives the positive focus of attention and gains the power to control the next episode of play. Social games are structured so that no prior skills or knowledge are required. There are no advantages to either sex, nor do speed or strength guarantee success over those weaker in these qualities. Individual success is guaranteed in the game whether the player succeeds or fails at avoiding becoming *It!* Additionally, all kinds of people can enjoy social games together—children and adults, the healthy and the impaired, the quick and the slow, the happy and the sad.

Social games are effective in arbitrating personal disputes. Social games can be effectively used to help people in a group resolve differences that naturally arise from close and prolonged contact. People tend to forgive and forget, let bygones be bygones, have the chips fall from their shoulders, and enjoy each other.

Most of the games in this book are very old, coming from societies where people lived in cohesive communities where the daily tasks were socially shared. Examples of such life-styles are early American pioneer settlements, African, Eskimo and Asian tribal villages, and European rural villages. The social game was probably developed and played because work relationships, being highly social in nature, caused friction and disputes that had to be controlled because people were interdependent economically and any serious social instability would threaten all. To maintain stability, these communities would gather in the village square or town hall and ritualistically engage in play, drama, dance, and song.

These people were not as alienated as we are today. Our society is weakening in community cohesion; our economics tend to drive us away from one another. The glorification of individualism, fierce competitiveness, privatization of social institutions, suburban sprawl, all provide little incentive or desire for getting along with others. The author feels we have reached a crisis in interpersonal relationships in the school as well as in the society at large. This book is offered as a practical resource to school personnel to aid in structuring positive school environments that will enable children to acquire the social skills necessary for learning.

A Big Wind Blows...

Objective
To focus positive attention on individuals.

Number of Players: 15 to 60

Place: Classroom or gym

Equipment: Chairs

Formation: Sitting in a circle of chairs. The *It* stands in the center.

Description: A chair-for-all-but-one-mixer game. One of a family of such games (see *Come Along, How Do You Like Your Neighbor?*, *Vegetarianism*, and *Fruit Salad*).

Action

The *It* player attempts to gain a chair at the expense of another player. He does this by calling, "A big wind blows for all those who...!" (Adding some quality). For example, "...all those wearing sneakers!" or "...all those in love!" All seated players who have the quality must leave their chairs and rush to find another chair and so does the *It*. The player left without a chair is the new *It* and continues the game.

Teacher's Guide

This is a great game to help students meet motor needs (escape the confines of their desks), while facilitating getting to know more about one another.

Initially children will most likely play to meet their motor needs and select superficial qualities such as clothing, but eventually they will become more sophisticated and call qualities that explore feelings and personalities like calling "...all those who *love* school!!"

The *It* role receives plenty of positive attention, and gives the student a chance to be creative and control the action. These fine qualities make this an excellent game to use to make students feel good about their classmates. It makes natural the mixing of students so they can expand the number of friendly contacts. This contributes to positive changes in attitudes and behaviors. Use this game at the start of the school term for early socialization benefits. It gets the class off to a friendly start.

Airport

> *Objective*
> *To heighten communication skills.*

Number of Players: 18 to 30

Place: Classroom

Equipment:* Blindfold, assorted objects like books, trash basket, box of tissues, etc.

Formation: Two lines of players facing inwards, spaced approximately 3 or 4 feet apart.

Description: A communication game.

Action

Players are divided in half and lined up, forming the two sides of an imaginary runway. Objects are arranged on the runway to eliminate a straight-through path. (The objects are imaginary buildings, power lines, etc.) Two players volunteer to be a pilot and a ground control navigator. The pilot is blindfolded (to simulate thick fog) and has to be guided through the obstacle course *without touching* any object. The navigator may not touch the pilot but may move around freely through the course to give verbal instructions only.

After either a successful or unsuccessful attempt, the pilot and navigator may switch roles or two new players selected.

Teacher's Guide

This activity is technically not a game. It is a communication exercise that is challenging and fun. It is used to highlight communication skills and to generate real experiences as a basis for discussing problems of being understood. Invariably, some navigators insist on using visual cues and do not realize how useless they are in communicating to a blindfolded person.

Most students get excited about the challenge of landing a plane in the fog without crashing, so getting volunteers is usually no problem.

* See *Game Kit* information on page 153.

Alibi

Objective
To highlight conflict resolution issues.

Number of Players: 13 to 25 active players plus an audience.

Place: Classroom

Equipment: Chairs, two tables, podium (optional), gavel, and a book to simulate the Bible (optional).

Formation: Tables and chairs arranged in a courtroom setting.

Description: Alibi is a simulation game (the only one in this book) that allows a great range of acting, spontaneous role playing, and sharp, intellectual exchanges. It can be played for entertainment or as an educational experience in conflict resolution.

The game can take a long time to play, but no one ever seems aware of time passing. You can play anywhere but the interior can enhance the performance—a rich wood paneled library being the most stimulating environment but the classroom is fine.

Alibi can be a complete embellished stage production but the rules and components offered here are basic. The barest game has a judge who serves as jury. The full cast game uses a 12 person jury plus the trial audience.

Action

A volunteer is elected to be the judge and the remaining group is divided in half. One half becomes the defense, the other the prosecution. The judge is now the leader of the game and the more leadership she has, the more smoothly run and enjoyable the game. A short time is allocated for the prosecution group to decide on a crime and a person in the defense group to be charged. A short indictment hearing is convened and the judge asks that the indictment be read. After the indictment, both groups meet separately and plan their case and choose who will be witnesses, as well as select their counsel. Both teams jointly decide on the number of witnesses to be called and cross-examined, and the number is based on the amount of time allotted (three is manageable).

The judge will convene the trial, call witnesses who are questioned and cross examined. Then the jury or the judge (if there is no jury) rules guilty or not guilty!

Teacher's Guide

Students enjoy this game if the witnesses are allowed to develop their characters succinctly by being asked a few simple questions as opposed to getting bogged down in an endless stream of questions designed to trap them. The game works best when the chosen roles are within the student's verbal ability. For example, a shy, quiet person would be miscast as the judge or prosecuting attorney, but would be just fine as a juror, spectator or character witness.

Ruling out the "Perry Mason ending"—the trick or forcing the real criminal to jump out of the audience confessing while attempting to escape the courtroom—helps make the game more of a thinking exercise.

Sometimes the issues raised during the simulation are hard to settle after the game is declared over. Arguments about the correctness of the ruling can go on for some time.

Our culture is so litigious and crime involved that children are knowledgeable about these issues and handle the social content of this simulation game well.

Alphabet Race

Objective
To teach cooperation, fair play and spelling.

Number of Players: 20 to 50

Place: Classroom or gym

Equipment:* Two sets of alphabet cards. 26 letters on cards 4 inches by 4 inches, preferably each set a different color.

Formation: Two teams in parallel lines, each facing a table with a set of alphabet cards spread out, face up. The leader moves from a position facing both teams, where he announces the word to be spelled, to a position between the teams facing the spellers, where he picks the winner of the round. The width of the playing area determines how large a word can be.

Description: A team spelling bee race.

Action

The leader calls out a word to be spelled (it should contain no double letters). For example, CAT! The first three players of each team, rush to their table, and pick up their proper letter (the first picks up the "c," the second the "a" and the third the "t"). No extra players are allowed at the table—just one player for each letter in the word. Players turn around to face their team and holding the cards chest high so the word is spelled correctly from left to right. The first team to display the correctly spelled word wins the point for that round. The cards are replaced face up on the table (no special arranging of the letters allowed!) And these players go to the end of their team and the players move up to the starting line. The first team to reach a set number of points wins the game.

Teacher's Guide

Teachers are always delighted when shown this marvelous spelling game and it's easy to see why. *Alphabet Race* is not only a social game but can also contain classroom subject matter. Many teachers feel guilty when playing a game with their students (not strictly state mandated) but this game is certainly school work!

Alphabet Race mobilizes most groups. It arouses excitement and team spirit which quickly overcomes anyone's fear of spelling. The team is responsible for success not the individual. Sometimes the competitive spirit is so strong that players start to scapegoat team members and it is helpful if the leader points out that it is a team effort and that maintaining team cohesion is the best strategy.

* See *Game Kit* information on page 153.

In leading the game, always point out that it is a coaching game where players may help each other spell, assist with finding letters and shout out advice. One player, a superior speller, is even allowed to tap and tell each player what letter they should find.

> **Tip**
> Sometimes it is a good idea to have players turn to their two neighbors and say, "I promise to do my best!" This lays a basis for not scapegoating, if they lose.

Alphabet Volleyball

Objective
To facilitate group building.

Number of Players: 15 to 20

Place: Gym or outdoors

Equipment:* One ball. Either a volleyball, playground or foam ball.

Formation: Cluster, standing.

Description: An informal volleyball game that rallies the group spirit.

Action

The leader hits the ball up and all the players chant the letter "A." The next hit is "B" and so on. The goal is to successfully hit the ball into the air 26 consecutive times until the letter Z! The ball must *not* fall to the ground. A person may hit the ball more than once but not twice consecutively. If the ball touches the floor or ground, the game starts again at A.

Teacher's Guide

This is a simple game that mobilizes group spirit. Players can choose their level of action and usually everyone gets caught up in the task and the spirit of the group's success.

Sometimes you will have to give a pep talk when many failures occur. You may also have to encourage everyone to chant the alphabet loudly because they may start to mumble softly. The chanting is a unique part of the group experience and actually helps in reaching the goal.

After experiencing group success, the players should feel more comfortable in the group and be ready to tackle other games or activities requiring trust and cooperation.

* See *Game Kit* information on page 153.

Balloon Burst Relay

Objective
Provide a humorous, cooperative outlet for aggression.

Number of Players: Up to four teams of twelve each.

Place: Classroom or gym.

Equipment:*   A chair for each team and (optional) a chair for each player. Inflated balloons for the number of rounds times the number of teams.

Formation: Teams in parallel lines facing an empty chair a running distance away.

Description: A cooperative team relay to see who is the fastest to pass and burst a balloon.

Action

Each team sits in a line and the first player is given a balloon. On the "go" signal, they pass the balloon to the next player on down the line until it gets to the "buster." That player rushes up to their empty chair, places the balloon on the seat and attempts to bust it with their rear end! First to do so wins a point for their team. A new "buster" is chosen and a fresh balloon given to each team for the next round.

Teacher's Guide

This game generates a tremendous amount of excitement and laughter. This is why I run it by rounds instead of continuously (it can get out of control). It is a wonderful combination of aggression, humor, cooperation and attention getting. I use it when younger children are very angry and aggressive, but too young to play *Swat*.

There are many variables to **Balloon Burst Relay**. How inflated the balloons are determines how difficult it is to burst them. Of course, the funniest moments are when bursting the balloon is a challenge. Teams can be organized by rotating seats automatically (if the game is run as many times as there are players on a team), or the last "buster" can choose the next and the game can be ended before every player has a change to be "buster." This method has the advantage of being sensitive to the fact that some players may be afraid of exploding balloons.

* See *Game Kit* information on page 153.

Bird, Beast, Or Fish

Objective
Strengthen nonverbal communication skills.

Number of Players: From 2 teams of 5 each, up to 6 teams of 15 each.

Place: Classroom, gym or outdoors.

Equipment: None

Formation: Team clusters equal distances from the leader.

Description: A pantomime team race game.

Action

Each team sends a player-actor to the leader. These individuals huddle with the leader, who whispers to them the specific name of a bird, beast or fish (like peacock, horse, shark, etc.). They immediately rush back to their teams, and act out the creature in *strict* pantomime (no sounds permitted). Their team-mates guess out loud the creature they think is being acted out. As soon as the player-actor hears the correct guess from one of his teammates, he dashes back to the leader. The team that guesses correctly and whose actor returns to the leader first wins the point. The game continues with new player-actors chosen each round, and lasts until one team reaches a preset number of points.

Teacher's Guide

The interactions created by playing this game are rich, humorous and beneficial to students because it fosters individual self-expression. Some actors get so deeply involved with their role that they forget to return to the leader to win the point!

Before playing, it is helpful to prepare a list of living things that are appropriate to the students or are part of the curriculum. The leader gets to observe just how accurately an individual student can communicate non-verbally and how they improve their acting over time. When playing with older students it may be wise to instruct players not to bump into the leader because the competition can be exuberant. Imagine getting run over by a charging rhinoceros!

Broom Hockey

Objective
To provide safe outlets for aggressive feelings.

Number of Players: 14 to 30

Place: Gym

Equipment: Two matching brooms (push or straw style), a knotted cloth (puck), and two chairs.

Formation: Two teams in lines facing each other twenty-five to thirty feet apart. A chair and a broom at each end of the room centered between the teams. The puck is placed in the center of the playing area. The length of the playing area depends on the number of players.

Description: A sideline hockey game.

Action

The teams count off consecutively starting at opposite ends. If the group is of mixed ages or sizes, they may be arranged by height before the count off. The leader calls a number and those two players rush out to opposite goals (leader designates which end), pick up the brooms, rush to the puck and try to sweep it under their goal (chair) which is opposite to where they picked up their brooms. The player who accomplishes this wins a point for his team and both players return the brooms and go to their place in line. Next round is started when the leader calls another number. The first team to reach a set number of points wins.

Teacher's Guide

This game and *Tire Pull* are the most aggressive and competitive games used in *Social Play*. The players are pitted against one another, matching speed, guile and strength. Most other *Social Play* games are designed to minimize physical prowess as an element of play. So why are they included!

They are included because *Social Play* is not merely a play experience. It is also a powerful learning system. The learning takes place in a social context.

Social experiences help children modify their behavior more than verbal exhortation does. As a socially conscious leader, you must offer students experiences by which they learn to deal with the repercussions arising from their actions. A leader must be able to meet a group at their level of functioning and many classes contain rough, angry students. This type of student does not readily take to Milquetoast activities nor does he quickly change into an obedient, mild mannered person. Therefore, the *Social Play* repertoire must include a wide variety of play experiences to effectively engage all kinds of students and situations.

Bull In The Ring

Objective
To provide for the safe expression of aggression and focus of attention.

Number of Players: 10 to 20

Place: Any

Equipment: None

Formation: Circle, players hooking elbows, with *It* in the center.

Description: A one-against-the-group escape game.

Action

The object of this game is for the *It* (bull) to break out of the ring of players. The bull may use any method to get out (such as cajoling, tickling, or battering). The ring players may not actively do anything to the bull (such as using their hands or kicking), but must attempt to keep the ring closed and prevent the bull from escaping.

After the bull escapes, a new bull is selected by volunteering or by picking one of the players who allowed the escape. The previous bull rejoins the ring.

Teacher's Guide

This game can be rough but doesn't have to be violent. I've seen kindergarten children play the game without any body contact—they just dart through players' legs. Adolescents often play roughly by battering away until someone gives in. Be sure to let the "bulls" know that they can use any way to escape (some others are: *It* asks a friend to let him out, offering favors or money, or faking a charge and backing out).

This game is contradictory in form and content. It provides intimacy (people holding onto each other), and allows aggressiveness (trying to batter people). A rough group may inadvertently become comfortable with touching because they are not conscious of their intimate proximity while they are acting aggressively.

Caboose Dodgeball

Objective
To provide safe outlets for aggression and teach cooperation.

Number of Players: 25 to 50

Place: Gym, multi-purpose room or outdoors.

Equipment:*   A foam ball, volleyball size.

Formation: Circle, standing, with three player train in the center.

Description: A social content dodge ball game.

Action

Three volunteers form a train inside the circle by holding waists. The first person (engine) is free to use his hands, feet and body to deflect the ball; the center person is the glue that holds the train together, and the last person (caboose) is the target that the ring of players are trying to hit with a ball.

The train maneuvers to keep the caboose person out of range of the ball. The ring can use any strategy (passing, lobbing, etc.) to hit the caboose. After a hit, the player who threw the ball becomes the new engine (front person) the engine person moves to the middle; the middle person becomes the caboose, and the caboose rejoins the circle. Or after a hit, all three players may go choose some one to go in their place (sometimes it is necessary to have boys pick girls and girls pick boys).

> **Tip**
> Using a space age non-peeling foam ball allows angry aggressive children to express their emotional intensity without endangering others. This is better than the leader trying to temper them.

Variations

Use two balls and, if the group is large, two trains.

* See *Game Kit* information on page 153.

Teacher's Guide

With good tactics, the circle players can maneuver the train out of position where even a softly tossed ball can hit the caboose. I always have the replacement train players take the place in the circle of the player they choose. This automatic mixing helps students experience others randomly *and* keeps them from choosing just their friends or gender.

The train formation of holding waists is intimate contact, which is sometimes uncomfortable for certain players. But when under fire from a whizzing ball, this factor is quickly overcome. This happens a lot in many grades where boys and girls have problems relating.

This game helps release pent-up aggression with a minimum of danger that the players will personalize such behavior. It also fosters cooperative relationships because the greatest pleasure in playing the game comes when the players are working well together.

> **Tip**
> If a child has trouble with touch-ing the opposite sex, you may ask them if they can tell a boys hand from a girls hand? If they say yes, they can blindfold them and have someone shake their hand and tell the class which it is!

Catch A Smile

Objective
To provide intimate proximity and friendly eye contact.

Number of Players: 20 to 35

Place: Classroom or gym

Equipment: Music that can be played and stopped in varying intervals.

Formation: Circle of players. Bridges formed by pairs holding hands above the circle.

Description: This game is taken from the old English children's play party elimination game, ***London Bridges***, in which the "bridge" falls periodically, capturing players who then become bridges.

Action

Two volunteers form the first bridge, by holding hands up high. When the music plays, players move around in a circle passing under this bridge. When the music stops, the bridge couple's hands come down. The person caught by the bridge waits until another player is caught and they join together as another bridge anywhere along the circle. This process continues until all players become bridges or until a single player is left.

Teacher's Guide

This is one of two games (the other is ***Fruit Salad*** that for some time I played only with younger children. Once I had tried them with adults, I was quite pleased to discover that it was just as much fun as with the young. This is proof that the leader's attitudes and biases limit his group's experiences; play the games and let the players decide what's fun!

Chain Pantomime

Objective
To develop nonverbal communication skills.

Number of Players: 15 to 30

Place: Any

Equipment: None

Formation: Sitting in a semicircle

Description: A whispering-down-the-lane dramatic game.

Action

Four volunteers are chosen and leave the playing area. While they are out, they order themselves into #1, #2, #3 and #4. The remaining group selects a dramatic action. This action is performed by a player in the group. For example, getting a flat tire and repairing it. All the action is done in pantomime.

The #1 volunteer is called back into the room and watches the original skit and is instructed to remember what he has seen so that he can reproduce it as accurately as possible for the #2 volunteer.

The #1 volunteer then performs the skit for #2. #3 is then called into the playing area and #2 performs the skit for #3 to watch. #4 is called in and #3 performs the skit for him. The #4 volunteer then gets three guesses as to what he thinks the original action was. Then #3 gets to guess, then #2, and then #1. The original may be repeated if the group is still absorbed in the action.

Variation

Whispering Down The Lane is the verbal version of this game. The first player whispers a descriptive statement to the next player who repeats it to the next and so on until the last player hears it and repeats what she hears. The original and final statements are then compared!

Teacher's Guide

The changes in the original skit when performed by #3 player can be as startling as in the verbal version of this game. What children perceive is a unique combination of objective reality, subjective reordering and memory loss. These are the factors which make this an astounding experience and gives the leader insights into personalities and how they process information and communicate non-verbally. The game is best enjoyed by groups who have patience and self-control because ad-libbing and unnecessary talking can ruin the concentration.

Sometimes this game is startling to watch, but at other times, if the skit selected is too obvious and provides few chances for misinterpretation, it can be a dud. When played well, it is an enriching experience. Chain pantomime gives players opportunities for dramatic expression in a social setting and simultaneously affords an entertaining spectacle for the nonactive players.

Chosen

> *Objective*
> *To increase powers of observation.*

Number of Players: 10 to 30

Place: Any

Equipment: None

Formation: Circle sitting on the ground, floor, or in chairs

Description: A power-of-observation guessing game.

Action

The *It* observes all of the players seated in the circle, and asks some of them to stand. Those selected to stand must have something in common that distinguishes them from those remaining seated. For example, the *It* may choose all who have blue eyes or have on belts. The *It* also stands if she also has the chosen trait. The seated players must then guess out loud what they think the chosen trait is. The standing players may speculate but they may only whisper among themselves. When the correct trait is guessed, a new *It* is selected.

Teacher's Guide

This game is an excellent choice for helping students to become more comfortable looking at one another. It provides an opportunity for students to actually look at peers without being critical. This is quite often a new experience for students in some schools where the wrong kind of glance might provoke a fight!

Chosen generates a great deal of curiosity. The players become excitedly involved in observation and deductive reasoning. Positive tension develops when players are not able to quickly figure out the chosen characteristic and resort to humor to fill in the void.

Sharpening skills of observation is very helpful in the education process and this game is a fun way of doing it. Observe the level of sophistication the players reach over a period of time as they become more familiar with the game.

Circle Kho

Objective
Provide focus of attention and high expenditure of energy.

Number of Players: 30 to 50

Place: Gym or field

Equipment: None

Formation: Circle of players, standing, alternately facing in and out. Two people not in the circle, one a chaser and the other the chased.

Description: A one-against-the-group tag game.

Action

The best way to explain this game is to compare it to the deer hunting method used by Central American Indians. The tribe would station hunters in strategic locations. One hunter would begin the hunt by chasing a deer, and when that hunter tired, he would steer the deer to the next fresh hunter. No weapons were used. The hunters would collectively chase the deer until it collapsed from exhaustion.

This is the premise behind *Circle Kho*. The first chaser (hunter) starts to pursue the *It* (deer) on the outside of the circle. If the deer player runs inside the circle, the hunter player *cannot run into the circle*, but must tap one of the circle players facing *inward*. This player now chases the deer while it runs inside the circle. If the deer runs out of the circle, the second chaser cannot leave the inside of the circle but must tap a player facing *outward*. Every time the deer runs into or out of the circle, a new chaser must be tapped to continue the chase until the deer is tagged by a hunter. The chaser who taps another chaser takes their place in the circle and faces in the same direction. After a successful tag, a new deer is chosen.

Teacher's Guide

Groups have initial difficulty in learning this game, and the leader should be patient. The game has a different twist from tag games normally played in our culture. The *It* (deer) will inevitably become exhausted and be tagged, but he can gain a feeling of accomplishment by avoiding being tagged for the longest possible time. It is a great challenge to "take on" the entire group—one against the world. The chasers usually experience early frustration because they do not achieve the level of cooperation required to quickly tag the deer player. They get confused about which way to run, where to stop or who to tap, thus giving temporary advantage to the *It*.

Coffee Pot

Objective
To provide opportunities to practice deductive reasoning.

Number of Players: 6 to 30

Place: Classroom or outdoors

Equipment: None

Formation: Sitting around

Description: A verbal guessing game.

Action

A volunteer *It* leaves the playing area and the group decides on a common activity like eating, sleeping, dancing, etc. The *It* returns and has three guesses to identify the activity. To gain information about the secret activity, the *It* asks when, where, and with whom type questions. When the *It* feels he knows the action, he uses one of his guesses. A sample round could go like this (*Eating* is the chosen activity):

"Do you Coffee Pot in the house?"......................"Yes"
"Do you Coffee Pot in the bathroom".................."No"
"Do you Coffee Pot in the kitchen?"...................."Yes"
"Do you Coffee Pot in the dining room?"..........."Yes"
"Is it *Eating?*"..."Yes!"

Teacher's Guide

This game is not strong in social content but it is relaxing and fun when groups have settled down and are relating well. Students who have not had their needs for attention and physical activity fulfilled will often behave impulsively when playing guessing games. They will not be able to sit still and enjoy listening, thinking, and observing, which are the qualities that make quiet verbal games pleasurable. The development of patience helps to increase the enjoyment of this guessing game.

Coin Relay

Objective
Provide experiences in team cooperation enlivened by competition.

Number of Players: 24 to 60

Place: Classroom or gym

Equipment:* Chairs for all plus one and four identical coins.

Formation: Four equal in number teams lined up in a perfect square, facing an empty chair in the center. Chairs should be close together, but there should be space between teams at the four corners of the square.

Description: A pass-the-object team relay race game.

Action

Coins are held up by the team member on the extreme right of each team. On a signal from the leader, coins are passed through every team member's hands, until it reaches the last player on the left. This player, with coin in hand, gets up and races clockwise around the center chair and returns to the chair on the extreme right of his team. While he is running around the center chair, his teammates move one chair to their left so the chair he returns to is vacant.

When he arrives, he passes the coin and the relay is repeated in this manner until every team member has run around the center chair and the team resumes its original order. The first team to do so and raise their hands wins.

If the coin is dropped, the team has to retrieve it and continue passing from the spot where it was dropped. No one is to touch or move the center chair.

Variation

Two or three teams can play when numbers are too small for a full square. The formations would be three sides of a square or two teams facing on opposite sides of the pylon chair.

* See *Game Kit* information on page 153.

Teacher's Guide

Coin Relay always arouses great group enthusiasm. The pressure of competition in the relay style grows greater as the race unfolds and causes a strong need for team problem-solving, cohesion and fervor. Many teams (mostly older student—not elementary) become devious—they may substitute a second coin, change sitting order to shorten the number of rounds or prematurely raise their hands as winners when they really have not finished. Never mention any of these practices if they do not occur because that may suggest their use! Most often, these "cheating" techniques will be done in a playful manner and will add a villainous aspect to the game. Honestly played, *Coin Relay* is as fine a social game as you will find. I use extra people as volunteer judges to help monitor the play and determine the winning, second, third and fourth place teams. These judges help keep everything orderly and within the rules.

Some legitimate forms of problem-solving include players stacking three or four hands in a hollow cone and passing the coin through all of their hands at once (doesn't break rule that coin must pass through every hand), or players chanting, "Shift!" when their player runs around the chair to keep all team members alert. Many times students become distracted by all the activity and are oblivious to their own team. This game has another element that I feel is an important experience for students today. That element is *organization*. There is much to be done in organizing for this game—four teams selected randomly, volunteer judges recruited, chairs arranged into orderly straight lines, etc. Students must be aware of their relationship to others throughout the game, particularly when running around the center chair simultaneously which is like driving around a New Jersey traffic circle.

For most Americans there are not many occasions (possibly a fire drill) or institutions (the armed forces and prisons) where they can practice group self-organizing. Nor are there opportunities when the general public feels safe in large groups because they are orderly, rather than disorganized and volatile. This game provides a safe feeling for students because there is organization.

It is good to run this game twice because the first time is a learning experience. In the interim, allow teams to discuss strategy and change the order of the team if they think it will help. When a player is not sure of what to do and makes a mistake, the team can become demoralized, but placing such players next to a helper improves the team's efficiency and minimizes the chances of anyone becoming a scapegoat.

If the group is young or impaired, use quarters; or larger coins, never dimes. And don't forget to have each player say to teammates, "I promise to do my best!"

Colored Squares

Objective
To focus attention and to teach delayed gratification.

Number of Players: 10 to 30

Place: Classroom or gym

Equipment:*   4" squares cut from multicolored construction paper or felt and two straight pins.

Formation: Sitting (with or without chairs) in a circle with a large play area in the center.

Description: A one-on-one, physical and verbal competition.

Action

Two volunteers stand facing each other, with hands held behind their backs. They close their eyes while one colored square each is pinned on their backs, between the shoulder blades. The leader then asks them to open their eyes and carry on a short conversation. Next they have to maneuver around attempting to see their opponent's color and defend their own from being seen. The first to see (no guessing allowed) and shout out their opponent's color, wins. Two new volunteers are then chosen to continue playing.

Teacher's Guide

This novelty game is a direct, competitive, one-on-one situation. It also furnishes qualities that compensates for the competition and produces more fun than a purely athletic contest. The audience participation enhances the attention getting, and the verbal exchanges are usually funny (players become shy about talking in the game and any utterance usually brings laughter). Another factor that makes this a valuable game is that young people love to play it. It think the attraction to this game stems a little from the competitive challenge but mostly from the students' instinctive realization that plenty of positive attention will be available.

* See *Game Kit* information on page 153.

There is added interest in playing ***Colored Squares*** when girls and boys compete. Boys and girls in the lower grades are close in physical ability and usually have a keen sense of the boys versus the girls competition, while older students feel a sexual self-consciousness from the inadvertent bumping (touch). You should be careful to pick players of similar height—much taller players have an unfair advantage over shorter ones. It also helps to enlist helpers, (I use adults and not students) to pin the colors. The issue of delayed gratification arises because the game is hardly ever played long enough for all students to be picked.

Come Along

Objective
To focus attention and broaden social contacts.

Number of Players: 18 to 40

Place: Classroom or gym

Equipment: Music source

Formation: Circle of chairs. Everyone sits except the *It* person, who stands in the circle. The music operator is outside the circle.

Description: A musical mixer game.

Action

When the music plays, the *It* walks around the circle and takes a player by the hand who comes along with him. This player now takes another player by the hand. Each newly selected player repeats the process so the chain of players grows while the music plays. When the music stops, these players drop hands and dash for empty chairs. The player remaining without a chair is the new *It* and begins another round when the music resumes.

Teacher's Guide

This is a charming, simple game. It has many comfortable playing levels and allows students to become fully active group members when they are ready. Being part of the game requires sitting in a chair observing others. Players who are not ready to mix, simply withhold their hands from the active players. Players eager to get into the action reach out hoping to be picked up. The leader may ask the sitting players to clap their hands to the music to increase the feeling of involvement. The choice of music affects the group's feelings too.

Dashing for chairs never fails to socially excite school children, and players become more excited when certain people become *It*—usually that person is the teacher (or it may be an extremely shy student)!

Early in this game the leader may have to remind the last player joining the chain to pick up another player—they often become awestruck by receiving so much positive attention that they temporarily lose sight of the needs of the rest of the players. If a player picks up with the wrong hand and becomes twisted, encourage them to extricate themselves so they do not get squeezed. When familiar with **Come Along**, groups of players may problem solve by holding hands while sitting so that when the lead player is picked they all get up! For the last round I always arrange for a long interval of music so that all players can be brought along so no one feels left out.

Dzien Dobry

Objective
This game is sociometric, meaning that playing it shows who is who in the group as to social standing. The game gives students a chance to hold their own among classmates.

Number of Players: 15 to 30

Place: Any

Equipment: None

Formation: A circle of players standing shoulder to shoulder facing inward with the *It* on the outside.

Description: This is the Polish version of a multi-cultural game (see the American version, ***Howdy Neighbor***) in which the *It* challenges another player to a walk-race around the circle. The last one back to the starting place is *It*.

Action

The *It* starts the game by walking around the circle, stopping to tap a player of choice on the shoulder. That player responds by turning out of the circle to face the *It*. The vacated space should remain open. The *It* bows and says, "Dzien Dobry" (pronounced *gin doe-bray,* which means "Good Morning") and the challenged player bows and says, "Dzien Dobry." Immediately, the players walk, *not run*, as fast as possible, in opposite directions around the circle. When they meet at the other side, they stop, hold hands, bend their knees and say, "Yak Sie Masz?" (pronounced *yock seh mush*, which means "How Do You Do?") three times. This should sound and look silly to the circle of players and is part of their enjoyment as spectators.

Following this action, the two players drop hands and continue walking in the direction they were facing, trying to reach the open space in the circle before the other player. The first to get into the open spot is safe. The other player becomes the *It* and starts another round of play.

Teacher's Guide

This game can arouse strong feelings. It has an intimate formation (close circle, arms touching), but its action is do-or-die competition, one-against-one, in full view of everyone. Failure to successfully problem-solve ***Dzien Dobry***, results in repeating the *It* role, and each repeat causes more exhaustion and frustration which leads to more failure. This phenomena can upset the entire group. They may feel sympathetic to the *It*, and rescue him or her, or they may gain pleasure in the *It's* misfortune and try to increase it.

This game will give you an accurate reading of the social relationships in the class. You may quickly find out who receives support from the class or who is the villain or bully. This knowledge may not otherwise be apparent in the day-to-day classroom routine which is a different social environment.

Feel free to substitute other languages.

Elbow Tag

Objective
To provide opportunities for attention, physical activity and intimate proximity.

Number of Players: 16 to 40

Place: Gym or field

Equipment: None

Formation: Paired players standing side-by-side, hands on hips and elbows hooked together. Pairs are randomly scattered in the playing area. Two players are free, one is the chaser (*It*), the other the pursued.

Description: A continuous action tag game.

Action

Simple tag is played between the two free players. If the *It* makes a tag, the roles are immediately reversed. To avoid being tagged, the chased player may run and dodge between the pairs or hook onto the free elbow of any player. At this point, the chased player and the player she hooks onto is safe, but the other half of that pair must now run away from the *It* or be tagged.

Quiz
All games are constructed out of only seven play elements! Tag is one, musical chairs is another—can you name the other five?

Variation: Bronco Tag

The pairs stand, facing the same direction, rear player holding the front player about the waist with the front player's hands free. The *It* chases the free player who must run into the arms of any front person to escape being tagged. When the front player grabs the pursued runner, the rear player holding the front player must now run from the *It*.

Teacher's Guide

Tag is as old as human society and is one of the seven basic play elements. These elements are like musical notes and all games are made from them. It is a universal form of play found to be popular in all cultures including other mammals. This is a particularly rich version of tag. *Elbow Tag* is one of my personal favorites because of its many interesting interactions and periods of intense enjoyment.

Several difficulties can arise in playing **Elbow Tag**. The game is difficult to understand, therefore players remain confused for a longer period of time than in most games. Some individuals cannot grasp the immediate reversal of roles and they find themselves retagged. Another problem arises when players respond only to their need to run free and circle the group several times, never thinking of hooking on and giving someone else a chance. This style of play meets individual needs at the expense of the group. Inactive players need to be entertained by active players, not ignored and left bored.

Because of these potential problems, the leader must always be ready to step in, stop the game, and demonstrate once again if there is confusion. The leader may have to shout, "Hook on, hook on!" to help increase the pace and involvement of the play. Another way to help make the game successful is shouting, "Freeze!" This stops the two active players, and then saying, "Reverse!" and reversing their roles. This technique gives a player who is having difficulty a chance to get out of being *It*.

El Tigre

Objective
To teach consensus and cooperation.

Number of Players: 16 to 40

Place: Any

Equipment: None

Formation: Two teams in opposing lines, four feet apart, switching into huddles at opposite sides of the playing area.

Description: This is the Spanish language version of a cross-cultural game, that involves a consensus process. This version has strong social and dramatic aspects that are expressed both in pantomime poses and in shared decision making. The American version is ***Rock, Paper, And Scissors***.

Action

There are three dramatic poses in the game:

1)   El Tigre (The Tiger)—Teeth bared, hands raised and held like claws.

2)   El Hombre (The Man or Mankind)—Arms crossed over chest with stern look on face.

3)   El Fusil (The Gun)—Arms thrust out as if holding a rifle.

Each team goes into a huddle and decides on which pose they will take. All team members must enact the agreed on pose or their team cannot win. After choosing a pose, both teams reassemble into opposing lines and the leader gives the signal to pose. A point is awarded based upon this hierarchy: El Tigre wins over El Hombre; El Hombre wins over El Fusil; and El Fusil wins over El Tigre. If both teams choose the same pose (a tie), no points are awarded. No spying is allowed.

Teacher's Guide

This game provides a powerful group process experience. Students learn to come to consensus which is an important democratic process. You will witness characteristics and relationships in your class— who is assertive, who is shy, who is a bully, who facilitates or who scapegoats. When a round is lost, is the team a good loser? All of these facets can be seen in the midst of fun and dramatic challenge.

Some students do not have the self-discipline to handle *El Tigre*. They will require you to program other games to assist them in learning the social skills that are necessary to cooperate with peers and handle losing in a game. When these abilities are present to some degree, *El Tigre* is one of the finest ways for them to enjoy improving them.

Elephant And Giraffe

> ### Objective
> *To tolerate and enjoy being silly.*

Number of Players: 30 to 60

Place: Gym or field

Equipment: None

Formation: Players standing in a circle, the *It* inside.

Description: A trick-someone-else-into-being-*It* posing game.

Action

The *It* goes up to any player, points to that player, and says, "Elephant" (or "Giraffe"). That player and two adjacent players must then assume the pose of an elephant (or a giraffe) before the *It* counts to ten. If any of the three fail to perform their part of the pose by the count of ten, that player becomes the new *It* and trades places with the old *It*, and the game repeats.

The poses are:

> *The Elephant*—The player pointed to makes two fists and places them on his nose like an elephant's trunk. Each adjacent player cups one hand behind the middle player's ears.

> *The Giraffe*—The player pointed to raises hands straight over head, stretching tall. Each adjacent player places one hand (thumb spread away from fingers) on middle player's waist.

Variations

Other poses can be designed, such as 1776—a fife player, a flag carrier, and a drummer. Or it could be monkey-see-no-evil (hands over eyes), hear-no-evil (hands over ears), and speak-no-evil (hands over mouth).

Teacher's Guide

The basic elements of this game are laughing at one's inability to do a simple task, and looking silly. Students need to be prepared to risk looking silly to get into this game, so the larger the group the easier it is. Mixed groups of children and adults makes for a looser, funnier session, too.

The *Its* are usually shy in the beginning but in a short while they count to ten lightning fast and become quite tricky in choosing an unsuspecting elephant or giraffe. There can be several *Its* at a time if the group is large enough. This game is a hilarious mixer!

Fibbing

Objective
Getting to know group members better.

Number of Players: 12 to 40

Place: Classroom

Equipment: Chairs for all players.

Formation: Audience sitting facing lone chair.

Description: A group interview game where the *It* is not allowed to tell the truth.

Action

Leader explains that every volunteer *It* must agree to answer every question directed at him but he must not tell the truth—he must lie! Players can ask any question. The *It* may step down whenever he wishes or when the leader excuses him.

Variation: Group Interview
In this version the *It* answers questions honestly, but may decline to answer questions he prefers not to answer (like, "Why are you so ugly?")

Teacher's Guide

Fibbing is an amazing experience. It is not so easy to lie spontaneously, when everyone watches. If the audience is clever, they can extract more information from the *It* when lying than if telling the truth. For example: Question—"Do you like the people in this room?" Answer—"I despise them!"

In our schools, it is easier for students to say that they don't like people than it is for them to admit they do, especially among fourth graders on up. I usually start Fibbing by asking the group, "Who has never told a lie?"

Fire On The Mountain

Objective
To provide focus of positive attention.

Number of Players: 29 to 59 (odd number necessary)

Place: Gym or field

Equipment: None

Formation: Two equal concentric circles standing. The inner circle faces inward, and the outer circle faces counter clockwise. The odd person *It* stands in the center.

Description: This is an African odd-person-out game, employing rhythmic sound patterns.

Action

The *It* starts the game by making rhythmic sound patterns by clapping, snapping, or stamping, etc., which the inner circle mimics. At this time, the outer circle moves counterclockwise around the inner circle. When the *It* is ready, he stops the rhythmic pattern, raises his arms high overhead and shouts, "Fire on the mountain!" The inner players also raise their arms while the outer players rush inside the inner circle and stand in front of an inner player. The *It* player also tries to stand in front of an inner player to avoid becoming *It* again. Inner players must not lower their arms until an outer player stands in front of them. When this happens they may lower their hands to their sides, or if players are friendly, on the new inner person's shoulders. The outer player who fails to find an inner player to stand in front of is *It*.

The game repeats with roles of inner and outer circles reversed (the original inner circle now becomes the outer circle and vice versa). Before each round of play, the players should be asked to step back because the circle always collapses inward.

Teacher's Guide

You must develop an effective style to teach *Fire On The Mountain* because non-Africans tend to have trouble performing multi-rhythmic patterns (similar to rubbing your stomach and patting your head at the same time). In addition, inner players often echo instead of simultaneously perform the movements of the *It*. Early in the game other difficulties may arise. Many *Its* do not understand that they are to find a partner in the inner circle and end up repeating the *It* role. Many times more than one player is left running around because inner players got confused and switched roles. Be patient during the learning period because *Fire On The Mountain* is a worthwhile and rewarding mixer game.

This game takes its name from an African fable. The fable is about a powerful tribal chieftain who conquers all of Africa. In his empire lies the highest mountain on the continent. He issues a challenge to all the warriors in his kingdom: "If you can stay on Kilamanjaro overnight without a fire, you will receive your own fiefdom with many wives." Over the years, countless, brave warriors attempt to stay atop the fierce mountain but none succeed. They succumb to the bitter cold and strong winds and suffer from frostbite and exposure. But one warrior comes along and succeeds. How? He has a friend build a fire atop the neighboring mountain and he keeps warm by watching it.

You may be amazed at either the creativity or clumsiness of the *Its* in performing their rhythmic patterns. The game takes on a special quality when the *Its* are musical and lead the inner circle in great sounding rhythms. Music teachers may stress this element of the game, but it is not necessary for an enjoyable experience. *Fire On The Mountain* is rich in self-expression opportunities and focuses a great deal of attention on the *It* role. It also helps students satisfy their needs for intimate proximity.

Front To Front

Objective
To provide intimate proximity and feelings of authority.

Number of Players: 15 to 35 (odd number necessary)

Place: Classroom, gym or outdoors

Equipment: None

Formation: Standing back to back, in pairs, person without a partner is *It*.

Description: An odd person out mixer game, based on anatomy and proximity.

Action

Players choose a partner and stand back-to-back. The *It* then gives commands—"front to front," "back to back," etc., causing the paired players to change their positions relative to each other. When the *It* is ready, he says, "change!" This signals all players to find a new partner. The *It* also finds a partner, leaving someone else *It*.

New partners can be gotten either by always starting back-to-back, or by assuming the same position they were in before the "change" command (for example, if they were standing back to back, they must find a new partner and stand back to back).

Variation: People To People
This version uses any body part, such as "toe to toe," "hand to shoulder," "cheek to cheek," etc.

Teacher's Guide

When used as an ending game, ***Front To Front*** always seems to solidify the good feelings developed during the session. I have never had it fail as an exciting way to enjoy the presence of other people. Children can initially be choosy and resist being spontaneous in selecting new partners, but this should diminish along with the nervousness about having the same or opposite sex partners.

The use of the variation makes for some interesting experiences in intimacy. When opened up to include any part of the anatomy, some *Its* invariably become mischievous and say "lips to lips!" You may choose to head this off by explaining the appropriate levels of intimacy at school. You may also suggest that the *Its* move the commands quickly (for example, not getting stuck at "hands to hands" for a long time) to minimize players becoming embarrassed, silly or disorderly.

This game highlights the positive value of *Social Play.* The *It* role carries with it power, control, and the focus of attention. What more could players desire! I sometimes end the game with "front to front" and have the players say, "I had a good time with you!"

Fruit Salad

Objective
To provide positive attention.

Number of Players: 20 to 40

Place: Classroom or gym

Equipment: Chairs for all but one.

Formation: Circle of chairs. The *It* stands in the center.

Description: A chair-for-all-but-one mixer game. One of a family of such games (see *How Do You Like Your Neighbor?, A Big Wind Blows, Vegetarianism* and *Zip Zap*).

Action

All players, including the first *It*, select a fruit and try to keep it a secret throughout the game. The *It* player tries to get a seat by one of two methods:

1)   The *It* can call two or more fruits, which signals everyone who chose those fruits to find another seat. The *It* attempts to get a seat during this exchange and the player remaining without a seat is the new *It*.

2)   Or the *It* may say, "Fruit Salad!" which means all players must find new seats. The *It* attempts to find a seat in this exchange and the player remaining without a seat is the new *It*.

Variation
Same as above, but the chair formation is random.

Teacher's Guide

When playing with younger children it may be necessary to go around and assign fruits by whispering to each player. Some may forget, but it will not matter. Students in traditional school settings usually relish *Fruit Salad* because it gives them opportunities to get out of their seats. Their enthusiasm is extremely high when "Fruit Salad!" is called. But many times I've had to remind the children that they must pursue an empty chair and stay in it because they tend to oscillate in the center of the circle trying to become *It*. This behavior should alert you that the students need more positive attention experiences.

At one time in my career I only led **Fruit Salad** with young children but by accident found that older students (and adults) like it too. Besides the thrill of dashing for empty chairs, older players enjoy a game within the game, that is, picking hard to guess exotic fruits (like persimmons, kiwi, kumquats, boysenberries, etc.) and trying to detect and expose the fruits of others. This adds intrigue to the game, but is usually too subtle for the younger set.

The picking of an obscure or common fruit is the way a player determines how physically active she plays (apples, oranges and bananas are most frequently called).

After the game, do a *go around* to find out which fruits were selected.

Go Around

Objective
To facilitate group building, increase listening skills and learning to respect peers.

Number of Players: 10 to 30

Place: Classroom

Equipment: None

Formation: Circle, sitting.

Description: *Go Around* is not a game. It is a democratic device to elicit information from all group members which is important for all to know.

Action

The leader composes appropriate questions and announces them to the group. If it is a new group, introductory items like *name*, *birth facts*, *favorites* and *interests*, are best. Everyone gives their answers in order around the circle. The leader makes it clear that each person is to be given the attention of all group members when they speak and that each speaker must talk loudly and clearly.

A *Go Around* can contain both factual and emotional questions.

Teacher's Guide

The structure of this activity is not a fun form. It requires many behaviors that are difficult to perform and control—politeness, patience, paying attention to others, and social awareness. The only obvious fun is in the content—a player says something consciously or unconsciously funny. But I discovered by listening to hundreds of students' recollections of *Social Play* sessions that they experienced *Go Around* as fun.

The reasons why students enjoy *Go Around* are:

1) Getting to know people is a strong and exciting human emotion. When subjectively individualized it is the process we call "falling in love." Our highly alienated life-styles limits getting to know people close to us (neighbors, classmates, etc.). People become highly defensive against expressing feelings to others for fear that personal information will be used against them.

2) It is a true democratic experience, where all students give opinions without rebuttal. No one

censures replies, and the teacher does not require a "correct" answer.

3)   It forms a basis for building a community. Everyone is introduced, informed of the group's goals and the leadership establishes social order.

4)   Social order and the focus of attention allows group members to feel comfortable enough to disclose things about themselves that more probing methods force underground.

5)   It satisfies everyone's need to be the focus of positive attention. This is important for both shy students, who in other activities may not be able to successfully compete for attention, and for overactive students who need help in refraining from talking too much.

Try not to take this seemingly simple activity lightly. The questions asked must be carefully tailored to the group and the situation. Questions that surpass the members willingness to respond will cause discomfort and lead to group failure. When **Go Around** is used with a group for the first time, questions must be nonthreatening and elicit enough information to accurately gauge the emotional level of the group and what issues it should tackle. I once asked a group of elementary school students, "What makes you happy?" One boy squirmed in his chair, sputtered, hunched his shoulders but gave no answer. I then said, in a humorously mocking way, because I assumed he was just shy, "You must never be happy." I then turned to the class and teased, "He's just an unhappy boy!" Later that day I learned that he was indeed an unhappy boy. His parents had been divorcing and struggling for years and he was presently seeing both a psychologist and a psychiatrist. I should have been more sensitive to the fact that children are often emotionally upset.

The phenomena of students recalling having fun during an activity that does not appear to be fun still intrigues me. It raises many interesting questions about human beings and their social environment. It also reinforces my hunch that people have in addition to their regular memory (a data bank of facts) a special memory whose content is made up of *social interaction impressions*. These memories help to enrich our mental attitudes.

Group Buzz

Objective
To build group cohesion.

Number of Players: 12 to 35

Place: Classroom

Equipment: None

Formation: Circle, sitting.

Description: A consecutive counting game based on substituting the word "buzz" for every number involving seven.

Action

The first player calls out, "one" followed by the next player in the circle who says, "two" and so forth until the counting reaches the seventh player who must say "buzz" instead of "seven." Each time the counting reaches a number containing seven or a multiple of seven, that player must substitute *buzz* for that number. Any player who says a *seven* number or says *buzz* if her number does not contain a *seven* must start the game over from *one*. The object of play is to reach fifty without making a mistake. The buzz numbers to fifty are 7, 14, 17, 21, 27, 28, 35, 37, 42, 47, and 49.

Variations: Group Reverse Buzz:

The same as *Group Buzz* with this change: When a player says "buzz," the direction of the counting reverses one count per buzz and then goes forward again (at 27 and 28 the reversing goes back two players before going forward). This version is more difficult than *Group Buzz* and is played after the group is functioning cohesively.

Teacher's Guide

Group Buzz is similar to *Alphabet Volleyball* in the group process but it has no physical component. It is hard for players to deal with the frustration they feel when mistakes are made in. This is because they can not rid themselves of these feelings quickly in a physical way and move on as they can in *Alphabet Volleyball*.

What has to be learned to be successful at this game is supporting the players who make mistakes instead of criticizing them. A group also has to keep itself alert and focused on its goal. These skills are difficult for many students because they are more experienced in not listening to and being openly critical of peers.

The play is usually intense and group failure can leave a bitter taste in everyone's mouth. Group failure feels devastating so use plenty of encouragement to prevent the group spirit from dissolving. On the other hand, there is no keener feeling than being in a group when it eventually succeeds!

When classes accomplish being supportive to group members, and show it in games, they will have progressed towards supporting each other in learning academic subjects as well.

Guard The Chair

Objective
To provide safe outlets for aggression and anger.

Number of Players: 20 to 40

Place: Gym or multipurpose room

Equipment:* A chair and a 8 1/2" foam ball.

Formation: Standing in a circle, *It* in the center with a chair.

Description: An old (played by the Pilgrims) mock goal-tending game.

Action

A volunteer *It* stands in the center guarding a chair. The players in the circle throw a ball trying to hit the chair. The *It* may use his feet, legs and body to deflect the ball from hitting the chair. When the chair is struck a new *It* is chosen.

Teacher's Guide

The critical point of **Guard The Chair** is that the players are supposed to be throwing at the chair. It is inadvertent that the *It* is struck by the thrown ball (the *It* sacrifices himself in protecting the chair). The content is therefore unintentional aggression. This dynamic is a healthy way to express feelings of anger. You may have to intervene if the aggression gets out of hand (the throwers may be throwing too hard or trying to hit the *It*).

The circle players must socially problem solve their task to successfully strike the chair. The initial play will usually be primitive and selfish, consisting of players holding the ball, feigning throws (which only gives the *It* time to recover) and then unleashing a cannon shot designed to penetrate the *It*. But with encouragement the circle should settle down to a strategy of getting the *It* out of position where even a softly thrown ball can hit the chair. High lob throws are interesting too.

* See *Game Kit* information on page 153.

Guess The Leader

Objective
To increase powers of observation.

Number of Players: 12 to 30

Place: Classroom or outdoors

Equipment: None

Formation: Circle, sitting or standing, the *It* leaves and returns to the center.

Description: This is an observation game which pits the group and its secret leader against the *It*. It is sometimes called ***Who Started The Motion?***

Action

A volunteer *It* leaves the playing area while the group selects a player who will lead them in a series of changing motions (clapping, snapping, waving hands, tapping feet, etc.). The players mimic this leader and change motions whenever he does. The leader tries to hide his identity from the *It*. The *It* gets three guesses to name who is initiating the changes.

Teacher's Guide

This game has a stunt quality, that is, the *It* doesn't know what the group knows. When incidents cause a reaction from the group, it is perplexing to the *It*. But the game works well if the group is friendly and the *Its* are inquisitive and competitive.

The *It* can be selected by the teacher or done automatically (present leader becomes the next *It*). The teacher-decided option is best when dealing with students who cannot handle the *It* role. When a class is functioning well, this game offers plenty of interesting interactions. The detection of facial cues, changes in sound and intuitive guesses by the *It* can be astounding to watch.

How Do You Like Your Neighbor?

Objective
To focus positive attention and provide harmless verbal outlets for hostility.

Number of Players: 15 to 40

Place: Classroom or gym

Equipment: Chairs for all but one.

Formation: Circle of chairs, with the *It* standing in the center.

Description: A chair-for-all-but-one mixer game.

Action

The leader counts off the group consecutively telling everyone to remember their number (the leader takes the last number). The object of the game is for the *It* to get a seat. This can happen in two ways:

1) The "I Don't Like Them" response. The *It* goes up to any player and asks, "How do you like your neighbors?" The answer is: "I don't like them!" The *It* then asks, "Who would you rather have as neighbors?" The answer given must be two numbers of the other players (for example, "one and fifteen!"). Instantly the two numbers called, and the two neighbors, must exchange chairs, and while this is happening, the *It* gets a seat. After the exchange, the player remaining without a seat is the new *It*. The two neighbors cannot exchange chairs between themselves. The person who is asked how he likes his neighbors does not leave his chair.

2) The "I Like Them Fine" response. The *It* asks the same question, "How do you like your neighbors?" The answer is, "I like them fine!" All players must change chairs, and the *It* tries to get a chair. The player remaining without a chair at the end of this exchange is the new *It*.

Variations

This is one of a series of games in which there is one less chair than people. See *Fruit Salad, Come Along, Vegetarianism,* and *A Big Wind Blows!*

Teacher's Guide

This game is loved by students. It quickly involves them in the group and allows them to vent disliking people, but in a socially acceptable, fun way. We all have feelings of dislike for some people but most of us will refrain from telling the person because we do not want to hurt their feelings. This game makes this difficult real life situation tolerable and fun.

It also provides for motor activity and focuses positive attention on the *It*. One caution is in order. Players wanting and needing attention may stand in the center of the circle forgetting to pursue an empty chair. If this phenomena takes place, the game should be stopped and the children reminded that they must pursue chairs. This behavior tells us that these children need more attention and their attempts to get it jeopardizes other's fun. This game is always a favorite among students (and mine too). I play it frequently and use it as a beginning game.

Howdy, Neighbor?!

Objective
To focus positive attention.

Number of Players: 40 to 70 (even number)

Place: Gym or outdoors

Equipment: None

Formation: Partner couples holding inner hands in a circle. The *It* couple on the inside of the circle.

Description: A large group, partner walk-race for the empty space game. The American version of *Dzien Dobry*.

Action

All players choose a partner and form a close circle. The *It* couple walks inside the circle until they meet a couple they want to challenge. They face that couple, bow, and say, "Howdy, Neighbor?!" The challenged couple bow and return the greeting. Immediately both couples start to walk in opposite directions (they should never reverse directions). Players may walk fast but may *not* run, drop hands, or cut corners. When the couples meet at some point across the circle, they stop, take four hands around, bend their knees and say, "How do you do" three times. After this exchange, they drop their opponents' hands, the *It* pair lifting their arms and the other pair dipping under to commence the walk race. The last couple back to the open spot is *It* and starts the next round.

Teacher's Guide

Howdy, Neighbor?! can be less than a success on some occasions. If the participants have not developed a tolerance or fondness for the group, the game can be overly rough or break down altogether. This happens when the players are strongly competitive and want to win more than they want to have fun.

One problem in playing *Howdy, Neighbor?!* is that it requires immediate intimacy in the form of hand holding. When working with junior high and high school players, the issue of young men holding each other's hands can cause a commotion. Having sexually heterogeneous groups is easier because players can pick partners with whom they are comfortable. On the other hand, elementary school children can react negatively to hand holding with the opposite sex. Mixed age groups (parents, teachers and students) are the easiest to get to hold hands and have fun at *Howdy, Neighbor?!*

When classes are not sufficiently sociable, the game is invariably played roughly. Hard collisions take place, partners separate and act as individuals, and the game deteriorates. The inactive players can no longer tell who is *It*, and the game has to be prematurely ended. This is a group failure that is not pleasant for the group or the leader. A second problem arises when players cut corners and run instead of walk. I usually let the circle monitor the play and decide when the rules are violated. My style is to ask the players in the circle to let out an "Ooooo!" when they observe these violations, and force the offending pair to repeat being *It*.

Enough said of the potential negatives. When ready for this combination of competition, cooperation, and intimacy, a group can experience fun equal to any other game. So many humorous and exciting interactions take place that every player, active or inactive, has a good time.

Human Tic-Tac-Toe

Objective
To teach self control and fair play.

Number of Players: 18 to 40

Place: Classroom

Equipment: Nine chairs

Formation: Two parallel teams in single file, facing nine chairs arranged in three rows of three chairs each.

Description: The famous two-dimensional paper/pencil game, translated to three dimensional team play.

Action

This game is identical to Tic-Tac-Toe played with pencil and paper, except that it is done with people as the X's and O's. One team is designated the "X" team and they cross their arms over their chests, while the second team is the "O" team, and they place both hands on their heads. The players do not have to hold their signs while they are standing in line, only when sitting in the chairs.

A coin is tossed to determine which team goes first. Their first player sits in a chair of her choice. The first player from the second team then sits in a chair of his choice. This continues until one team wins Tic-Tac-Toe by having three players seated in a row, either straight or diagonally. Ties do not count.

After each round, the active players get up and go to the end of their team and the players move up to the starting line. *There is no coaching or talking in this game.* Each player is on his own and makes his own decisions. The score needed to win is set by the leader.

Teacher's Guide

This game gets intense. It is difficult for players not to interfere by coaching active players. Sometimes they just blurt out, "No! Not there!" or they squirm so noticeably that the deciding player knows that something is wrong. This challenge makes **Human Tic-Tac-Toe** a good practice activity for developing impulse control (like "I'm thinking of a word that rhymes with..."). Another possible reason for the intensity in this game comes from anticipation of the euphoria experienced by the winning team and the dejection felt by the losers. It is difficult for players to deal with team defeat when individuals cause failure. These players often face a hostile team after making a poor choice. A class that can positively and successfully deal with acceptance of group members regardless of their performance shows a high level of social behavior. This high level should be a goal for all classes.

The most fascinating facet of this game is observing the diverse range of abilities to 'read' three dimensional space. Some children glance at the formation of players and instinctively go for the correct chair. Others study long and hard and still make an obvious wrong choice. There is little crossover between abilities to play two-dimensional Tic-Tac-Toe and this three dimensional form. The presence of people in chairs with everyone scrutinizing their choices makes a highly charged *four* dimensional climate. The key to success is a team's ability to hold together and avoid becoming critical of players.

I'm Going To California

Objective
To provide positive attention, increase listening skills and learning to respect peers.

Number of Players: 15 to 30

Place: Classroom

Equipment: None

Formation: Circle, seated.

Description: A rigmarole game (responses are repeated and added to).

Action

First person says, "I'm going to California and I'm going to take my (filling in an object of choice like an umbrella)." Second person says, "I'm going to California and I'm going to take my umbrella and my (he adds an item, such as "my pet dog")." The third person says, "I'm going to California and I'm going to take my umbrella, my pet dog, and my (whatever)." This process goes on until the last player repeats all preceding items!

Variation: Pantomime Version

The same action as in the verbal version, only the responses are acted out instead of spoken. "I'm going to California" are the only words spoken.

Teacher's Guide

A rigmarole game can initially cause anxiousness in some players because it tests recall ability and they fear they won't remember. However, do not lead the game like it is a psychological test; lead it in a manner so the players enjoy its humorous qualities.

When leading the dramatic version I have always been fascinated at how different players interpret the same item. For the same motion some actors barely lift a finger and others wave an entire arm. How each individual uniquely perceives and acts on his environment is an interesting way to gain insight into, and enjoy, their personalities.

I'm Going To California is also a game in which the group members get to know each other better. We can begin to better judge the needs of students that we see take instruments of violence instead of pets, toys and grooming utensils.

I'm Thinking Of A Word That Rhymes With:

Objective
To receive positive attention, gain impulse control, and express dramatic creativity.

Number of Players: 20 to 60

Place: Any

Equipment: None

Formation: Informal circle, sitting.

Description: A pantomime guessing game using rhymes.

Action

The *It* person chooses a one syllable word and tells the group a second word that rhymes with it. The object of the game is for players to guess the secret word. For example, the *It* chooses "gnat." The *It* says, "I'm thinking of a word that rhymes with 'cat' (hint word)." Whenever players think they know the word, they raise their hand. If selected by the *It*, they stand and *pantomime* their guess! No one is ever allowed to call out a guess. The *It* person has to guess the word the player is acting and state whether or not it is the secret word. If the word is not the secret one, the *It* says, "No, (says the word) is not my word!" and picks another player. When a player acts out the secret word, the *It* person must say, "Yes, (says the word) is my word." The game starts over with another *It* and a new word.

If the *It* does not know what is being acted out, other players who think they know can go up and whisper their guess to the person doing the acting. If their guess is incorrect, they sit down. If the guess is correct, they help act out the word. This goes on until the *It* person guesses the word being acted out.

Teacher's Guide

When playing this game with younger children be aware that they may select words that don't rhyme. So you may have to screen some choices to make sure there is a rhyme.

When I lead this game my goal is to encourage the students to express themselves in front of peers. It is good to have this in mind and guide the play towards creativity rather than on guessing. I have played *I'm Thinking Of A Word That Rhymes With:* with as many as twelve players performing a two act skit to describe the word. The game is perfectly balanced between the *It* and the other players. The *It* may have a secret, but she must guess what the others are acting and that is not always easy.

This game trains students in impulse control. Many will blurt out the first thing that comes to mind or raise their hands before they have anything to say. The game will also counteract the effects of passivity and stilted communications caused by watching excessive amounts of television and the habitual playing of video games. What is good and positive about the game is that it demonstrates that children like to act and communicate if given an opportunity. Students always love to play *I'm Thinking Of A Word That Rhymes With:* So do I!

In Plain View

Objective
To provide practice in self control and honesty.

Number of Players: 8 to 25

Place: Classroom

Equipment: Small object such as a rubber eraser.

Formation: Sitting in a circle, and milling around in the play area.

Description: A hide and seek game in which an object is hidden where it is visible.

Action

The *It* asks all the players to close their eyes while he hides an object somewhere in the play area. The object must be visible, and never concealed. The *It* then returns to the circle of players and asks them to open their eyes, stand up, and search for the object. If someone sees the object, (they may not expose it), he returns to his seat. The game continues until everyone has returned to their seats. Then a new *It* is selected to hide the object.

Teacher's Guide

This game gives life to the old saying, "If it was a snake it would have bitten you." The game highlights poor observational skills when under social or internal pressure (like not being able to find earrings on a dresser when late for a date). But the game is not all pressure; it contains humor and gives positive feelings to those who are sharp and clever.

The crucial issue raised in playing *In Plain View* in the classroom is that of trust. But do not raise the issue unless it comes up during the play; otherwise you may be giving the players ideas they may not have realized. Peeking and being accused of peeking can destroy the fun, and hopefully the students will learn that fun is a valuable experience and will act so as not to jeopardize it. It is also a good idea not to assign *Its* by making the first person to see the object the next *It*. Keep the options open.

In The Manner Of The Adverb

Objective
To learn the meaning of adverbs and nonverbal communication skills.

Number of Players: 15 to 40

Place: Classroom

Equipment: None

Formation: Informal circle, sitting.

Description: A dramatic guessing game, where the players help the *It* by their acting skills.

Action

A volunteer *It* leaves the room while the group decides upon an adverb (any word that describes an action and usually ends in "ly"). For example, "quickly" is chosen. When the *It* returns, he asks any group member to perform a specific action (brushing teeth, dancing, etc.) in the manner of the adverb. In this case, the person chosen would pantomime brushing his teeth quickly. This process goes on until the *It* guesses the adverb. The *It* gets three guesses, but has unlimited chances to ask players to act.

Teacher's Guide

This game has a well balanced structure. There seems to be a conspiracy against the *It* by the group but the *It* holds the real power. The *It* has no time restraints and can make every player act out any action he or she chooses (without realizing this, adolescents will pick sexy adverbs). Those doing the acting are really helping the *It* by communicating information about the adverb.

There is also balance in the difficulty between the *It* guessing and the players acting. If the group picks a difficult or subtle adverb for the *It* to guess, it is also difficult for them to act. These elements are not usually evident to the first few *Its* but later *Its* will learn these complexities. If the group is large enough, two people can be *It* and share in the deduction, guessing and coming up with things to ask. You should try to get the group to use easier adverbs during the first few rounds before moving into more subtle ones. If this is done nearly all *Its* will be successful.

This game will get students to understand adverbs a lot faster than weeks of grammar lessons.

Jerusalem Jericho

Objective
To provide the focus of attention and power to individuals.

Number of Players: 20 to 60

Place: Gym, multipurpose room or outdoors.

Equipment: None

Formation: Circle, standing, *It* in the center.

Description: An *It* versus the group game in which the *It* has power to control but is surrounded by unruly subjects.

Action

The *It* bows and says, "Jerusalem" and every player must bow at the same time. If the *It* sees a player not bowing, she makes that person *It* and trades places.

The *It* may also bow and say, "Jericho" which means players must not bow. If the *It* sees a person bowing to "Jericho," she makes him *It*.

The *It* person selects who is to be *It* if more than one person is caught.

Teacher's Guide

This game has many levels of action. The simplest level consists of players trying to bow or not bow at the right times. Sometimes that is difficult because the *It* can be tricky by slurring her pronunciation of the beginning sounds of the two words, "Jerrr..." and then quickly saying either ending. Or the *It* may get a player to mimic her bow when she says, "Jericho," by focusing on a person and bowing so quickly that she induces a reflex action. There is also the mesmerizing affect of a long series of Jerusalem's followed by a sudden Jericho.

But some of the "deeper" levels of the game take place when players try to get away with doing the opposite action of the *It*. Some players brazenly defy the *It* but seem to be invisible to the *It*. The *It* does not detect the not bowing to Jerusalem or the bowing to Jericho *even though they are standing face to face*.

Players watching this phenomenon can't believe it and often point an accusing finger at their fellow player and say, "Ooooh, she didn't bow!" But fellow players do not determine who is made *It* and the game continues. When the players become confident, the *It* usually becomes more paranoid and will start to rotate quickly to catch the suspected, mischievous players.

Some *Its* are shy and easily intimidated by playfully dishonest participants who say, "Who me? I bowed!" when they didn't. Often a moral mood comes over the group and they actually demand justice and try to make the devious player *It*. Sometimes this game reaches hilarious highs and at other times it's a dud. Hope all of yours will be successful ones.

Jump Stick Relay

Objective
To use competition to spur cooperation.

Number of Players: 20 to 60

Place: Gym or outdoors

Equipment:* A broom, baton or stick for each team.

Formation: Single file teams in parallel lines.

Description: This is an active relay, fostering cooperation among team members and competition between teams.

Action

On the "Go!" signal, the first player of each team races with stick in hand to a baseline (a wall, a fence or a line on the ground), touches it with the stick, runs back to her team, and hands one end of the stick to the second player while retaining the other end. These two (second and first) players on each team lower the stick and sweep down their teams, and all players jump over the passing stick. The first player stays at the end of the team while the second player races with the stick back up to the baseline, touches it, and then back to the next person in line (third team member). The second team member repeats the jump stick sweep with the third team member. This process continues until the last player does his sweep (with the first player). When they finish the last player stays at the end of his team while the first player takes the stick and rushes to the front of his team (not to the base), and raises the stick followed by the entire team raising their hands to signal they are finished. The first team to do so wins.

Teacher's Guide

Relays in *Social Play* repertoire must not be based on prior skills or physical prowess. This allows for social problem solving to take place and restricts the influence that speed has on determining success. Straight relays like the 4 x 100 meter dash, which is based on speed, are not suitable for inclusion in *Social Play* sessions.

Jump Stick Relay has the necessary social content yet it appeals to players with good physical abilities.

*** See *Game Kit* information on page 153.

You may exert some control on the amount of endurance and speed involved by varying the distance to the base. Of course, players with great speed but little sensitivity to others can be a hindrance to their teams by sweeping too fast and high.

This relay uses lots of energy and requires concentration. It arouses enthusiastic competition among teams. If, in their zeal, players sweep too high, they increase the chance that someone may not jump over the stick (maybe on it instead) and slow down their teams. Team members may be heard screaming, "Lower!, Lower!" when trying to prevent this. The ingredients of ***Jump Stick Relay*** add up to a rousing, well-balanced and physically active relay with suitable social content for helping players become more socially aware and have fun cooperating with classmates.

Kangaroo Relay

Objective
To provide a humorous cooperative experience.

Number of Players: 20 to 60

Place: Gym or field

Equipment: One playground, volley or basketball per team.

Formation: Teams in single file parallel lines.

Description: This is a humorous, team relay contest which relies little on prior known skills.

Action

The relay starts with the first player in each team passing the ball back to the next player, and so on, until the last player receives the ball. That player steps out of the team and places the ball between their knees, places hands on hips, and hops to the front of the team. This process repeats for all players until the team returns to its original order. The first team to return to its original order wins. If the ball is dropped during the relay it has to be retrieved and the action continues where the ball was dropped.

Variations
The pass can be over heads, through the legs or alternate over and under.

Teacher's Guide

This relay is included in the *Social Play* repertoire because it levels out prior skill advantages of players. Seldom do people practice squatting, hopping around with a ball stuck between their legs (many times the ball pops out from between the legs) making like a kangaroo!

Kangaroo Relay does an excellent job in helping people relax and loosen up around one another by acting and looking silly. The competition between teams is sufficiently strong to overshadow any feelings of self-consciousness. Leaders of this game get a bonus by not being players—they get to witness some very funny sights!

Last Couple Stoop

Objective
To provide friendly outlets for competitive feelings.

Number of Players: 30 to 50

Place: Large room or gym

Equipment: Music source

Formation: Partners, shoulder to shoulder into two opposite facing circles. Extra player to work the music. Judges stand on chairs.

Description: An active elimination musical game.

Action

Each couple stands shoulder to shoulder facing opposite directions, one in the outer circle, one in the inner circle. When the music starts, they move forward (one partner moves clockwise, the other counterclockwise) away from their partner. When the music stops, they must locate their partners, rush to them, take both hands and stoop (squat). The last couple to do so is eliminated from active play to become judges who help decide subsequently eliminated couples. Play continues until one couple is left and is declared the winner.

Variation: Hook Up
Same action except couples have to hook elbows back to back and stoop (squat), a more physically demanding version. Or partners may just take two hands (or hug) and remain standing.

Teacher's Guide

This is a rousing game! It can be rough, too. (For the first round you may wish to stop the music when the couples are close by and not on opposite sides of the room.) Competition and the threat of elimination forces some players to make risky moves that can result in collisions with other players. With some groups it is advisable for the leader to forewarn the players to be careful. In most cases, after the first mammoth collision in the center of the circle, players quickly learn to avoid future contact.

The elimination component (usually a *Social Play* no-no) of this game is modified so that players are not excluded from the game but change roles. They are asked to judge who is the next last couple to stoop. In other words, they are rewarded with a role of power. Some players realize it may be advantageous for one's health and energy reserves to be eliminated from the active play and become a safe, powerful judge.

The choice of music helps set the tone of the interactions. Livelier music sets a more spirited mood in marching around the circle. Hand clapping and dance steps can be encouraged too.

Lemonade

Objective
To sharpen nonverbal communication skills and provide physical outlets.

Number of Players: 30 to 60

Place: Gym or field

Equipment: None

Formation: Two parallel opposing lines.

Description: This is a combination dramatic, active, pantomime and tag game.

Action

Field or gym is marked off with a center line and two safe lines, one for each team approximately 15 giant steps from the center line. The game starts with each team standing behind their safe lines. One team, in this example the first team, starts the action by huddling and deciding on an occupation, let's say, carpenter. When ready, both teams line up arms over shoulders facing the opposing team.

The first team starts the action by taking three giant steps forward while chanting, "Here we come!" The second team takes two giant steps forward challenging with, "Where from?" The first team now takes two giant steps forward and responds with, "New York!" The second team, taking three giant steps forward asks, "What's your trade?" Then the first team takes two giant steps forward and counters with, "Lemonade!" The second team answers with, "Well, show us some if you're not afraid!" This time the second team takes as many steps as necessary to close the gap between teams to approximately two feet at the center of the playing area. The chanting is done to the steps taken, one step per word or syllable except when the final adjustment steps are made.

At this point the players bring their arms down so all of the players on the first team can begin to individually pantomime the team's selected occupation (carpenter, in this example) and the second team starts to guess out loud what they think the first team is doing. When the first team hears someone on the second team yell, "Carpenter!" (the correct guess) the first team immediately turns and races for their safe line before someone on the second team tags them. All players tagged before crossing their safe line are captured and must join the opposite team and become loyal players for that team in the next round. Both teams reassemble at opposite ends of the playing area and reverse roles. This time the second team selects an occupation and begins the chanting. There is no formal ending or winner—the leader ends the game while it is still fun.

Teacher's Guide

This is a fine game which blends many different play elements—dramatic expression, suspense, guessing and tag. You couldn't ask for more. The game utilizes chanting, a social form of expression that gives individuals a sense of belonging in the group. This experience helps students extract feelings of acceptance, trust and safety from the group. These feelings help to build individual self esteem.

The game has an ebb and flow, free-form structure that blends friendship, consensus and competition into a marvelously friendly atmosphere. No one cares who wins because there is usually no clear cut winner or loser. And in today's world, that is refreshing!

Line Tug Of War

Objective
To provide safe outlets for aggression and excess energy.

Number of Players: 16 to 30

Place: Any

Equipment: None

Formation: Two teams facing each other across a center line (chalk, tape, or imaginary).

Description: An ebb and flow, ropeless tug of war.

Action

The object of the game is for one team to pull all opposing team players across the center line onto their team. This is done by grabbing opposing players, and pulling them across the center line. When players are pulled across, they cease resisting and become loyal team members of their new team. Players can be involved in pulling for both teams many times.

Anyone who inadvertently steps across the center line is automatically on that team. Special challenges can also be negotiated within the general melee. Any number of players can join together to pull one player.

Teacher's Guide

This tug of war has a different tone than the traditional rope-pulling tug of war. People interact directly through touch. The interactions take place in many ways and combinations, and loyalties are constantly switching. The game is a veritable social stew, mixing together many social ingredients: face to face competition, physical challenge, rough touch, physical exertion, exhaustion, sense of belonging, immediate acceptance, and team strategy. Because of the variety of interactions offered in this game, it can serve the needs of all players. Here are some uses for the game:

1) To allow students to expend energy quickly and succinctly (the energy use in this game is on par with shoveling snow). This prepares students to settle down for sedentary activities.

2) To allow a group to experience competition without suffering the sting of losing (or winning) at the end of the game. When the playing is over, every one ends up on the winning team!

3)   To allow students to express aggression, without reinforcing it. The game does not support or value the player who wins or who is the strongest, most aggressive person.

Precautions may need to be taken when playing this game, depending on the group's exuberance and the physical environment. When playing indoors, make sure there are no dangerous, sharp or blunt objects in the path of the players. Also, warn players not to pull hard and then suddenly let go of another player, nor drag a person after they have crossed over the center line. Also, jewelry should be removed to avoid breakage or injury. People will occasionally experience superficial scratches on the hands and wrists when playing this game, but I haven't met anyone who seemed to care, nor have I ever seen anyone hurt more seriously than that.

Manito

Objective
To encourage and practice giving and receiving.

Number of Players: More than 15.

Place: Entire School

Equipment: Strips of paper in a hat.

Formation: Starts together in a group.

Description: A noncommercial, non-Christmas, Pollyanna game where favors and presents are given secretly until the time when all mystery Manitos (do-gooders) are revealed.

Action

Every player's name is written on a strip of paper and placed in a hat where each is picked and kept secret. The name picked becomes that player's Manito, and the object of the game is to secretly provide favors or gifts to that person during the interval the game is to be played. The gifts and favors may be sent by courier, placed where the Manito will see them, etc. The gifts and favors can be material (for example, candy), literary (for example, a poem), services (for example, carry one's books), or musical (for example, serenade). On the last day the entire group assembles and all Manitos are revealed. (See song below.)

Teacher's Guide

This game is used to get people to do nice things for others and have them learn to accept comfortably such favors and compliments. This kind of investment in others always pays human dividends.

The best Manito I've ever done took place over a three day period. The exchanges in that group were clever, creative, and loving. I still have some mementos that I received (one is a poem mounted in a handmade fancy frame). I remember groups of twelve people assembling around one Manito at lunch time and serenading them with a song. I remember the blushing of the receiving Manitos as a public display of their gifts were made and the accompanying "oohs" and "ahhs" of the crowd. This phenomenon happened for nearly everyone. One act was seemingly more creative than the preceding one. The suspense was awesome as students wondered who could possibly care this much for them as to arrange these most disarming showers of affection.

In our culture, these episodes are rare indeed. Exchanges of affection to peers must be carefully thought out or they may never take place. Normal commerce between peers usually is critical, negative and obligatory. This game structures the environment so that all the players feel good in making someone else feel good and the feelings escalate. I personally abhor Christmas Pollyannas, but I love Manito.

Manito Song

Manito, manito, manito, mine (2 times)
I wonder who you are
You are so nice to me
Manito, manito, mine.
I love my manito, yes, I do (3 times, slowly)
I love my manito, but I won't tell who (faster)

I've got a feeling warm and gay
As my manito casts his (her) name someday
But who he (she) is I will not saaaaaaaaaaaay

(Repeat the first stanza.)

The reason there is no tune to the song is that the song that I learned was too awful to sing. So you may compose your own or do without a song accompaniment during the revealing ceremony.

Pass A Smile

Objective
To receive intimate proximity and diffuse anger.

Number of Players: 10-35

Place: Classroom

Equipment: None

Formation: Circle

Description: Not technically a game, but a nice closure activity after a successful game session.

Action

First action: Leader turns to the player on the right and frowns. This player turns and frowns at the person on her right and so on around the circle. The frown must be *mean looking*.

Second action: Leader now smiles to the person on the left and that person passes the smile to the left, until all have received and passed the smile. The smile should be genuine and not fake.

Variation

Pass a smile without the frown.

Teacher's Guide

I "invented" this closure activity while working with older adults who sometimes appear like they haven't smiled or laughed for a long time.

The reason for the frown portion of this activity is to set up the smiling part.
Children often will have trouble accepting a smile if they still retain some unfriendliness or hostility (like relating to the opposite sex). And you must encourage the players to really frown (play acting) and smile (genuine) and not revert to "phony" smiles or frowns that look happy.

More and more attention is being paid to humor—smiling and laughing—by researchers as a human activity that protects people from illnesses. So, leading children in this positive and simple activity may bring them added future benefits.

Predicament

Objective
To provide deductive reasoning experiences.

Number of Players: 10-35

Place: Classroom or under a tree.

Equipment: None

Formation: Sitting around.

Description: A verbal guessing game.

Action

The first *It* volunteers to leave the playing area while the rest of the players decide on a predicament, for example, you've jumped from an airplane and your chute fails to open! The *It* returns and asks any player, "What would you do?" They respond with their opinion, for example, they may reply "I'd pray!" The *It* must try to deduce the original predicament and gets three guesses to do so. There is no limit to the number of players the *It* can ask. A sample game may go something like this:

> The group picks: "You jumped from an airplane but your parachute failed to open!"
> The *It* asks four players (or more), "What would you do?"
> 1st Player answers: "I'd pray!"
> 2nd Player answers: "I'd try the emergency one."
> *It* guesses: "Are you in an elevator that's falling?"
> Group answers: "No!"
> 3rd Player answers: "I'd close my eyes and review my life."
> 4th Player answers: "I'd aim for a river."
> *It* guesses: "You jumped from a plane and your chute failed to open?"
> Group answers: "Yes!"

Teacher's Guide

Predicament is a game that is fun and comfortable to play when a class is orderly, well-behaved and capable of listening to each other.

The enjoyment of **Predicament** lies in the fact that players are very clever and sometimes humorous. The *It* feels great when his deductive logic is sufficient to solve the riddle.

Pressure Nouns

Objective
To improve functioning under social and time pressures.

Number of Players: 8 to 25

Place: Classroom

Equipment: Any small object easy to pass (pen, key, etc.).

Formation: Circle, sitting.

Description: A time-pressure, word performance game.

Action

The first *It* stands in the circle and hands an object to a player of his choice. That player says the letter "A" and passes the object to an adjacent player, who says "B," and so on through the alphabet. When the *It* decides to, he points to a player who has spoken the last letter. For instance, the *It* points to the person who has just said the letter "I." That person continues to pass the object but letters are no longer spoken. Immediately, the letter "I" player must name six nouns (no proper nouns allowed) beginning with his letter "I." He must complete the list before the object is passed completely around the circle back to him. If he does not name six nouns in time, he becomes *It*, but if successful, the original *It* remains *It* and starts the game over again.

Variation
The number of nouns can be adjusted, based on size and the ability of the group.

Teacher's Guide

I use this game to understand social group dynamics as well as to have fun. I like to examine the sociometric structure of the group—who has power, who is well liked, who is disliked, etc., so I can better program other games. Sometimes players will help the chosen person by suggesting nouns out loud because they feel sympathy for the struggling player.

I also use this game to highlight how time pressure affects performance by relating it to the feeling of having to answer difficult essay examination questions with limited time. This is often an unpleasant experience, but an ample amount of enjoyment is supplied through the interactions in this game. For

107

example, silly sounding words are sometimes blurted out, or funny stuttering results when the chosen person's mind fails them just before the object arrives. Another interesting characteristic of this game is the role of *It*. Who is actually *It*? The designated *It* or the chosen letter player? The pressure is not on the *It*, although he has control of the game and receives attention. The *It* is actually a dual, shared role.

Pris

Objective
To provide vigorous outlets for aggressive feelings in a highly organized social form.

Number of Players: 20 to 50

Place: Gym or field

Equipment:* A foam ball.

Formation: Two opposing teams separated by a center line with a prison box behind each team.

Description: A combination of *Dodge Ball* and *Prisoner Base* in which one team tries to capture all opposing players by striking them with a thrown ball.

Action

The flip of a coin determines which team gets the first throw. A player can go up as far as the center line and throw the ball at players on the other team. If the ball strikes a player *and falls to the ground*, they are captured and must cross the center line and stand in the opposing team's prison. The players who are targets have two options—they can dodge or catch the ball. If the ball misses them they are safe. If they catch the ball, they can throw it at players on the opposing team. No player is captured when she successfully catches the ball, or if the ball strikes her but is caught by a teammate before it hits the ground. If the ball is thrown (on purpose or by accident) over or through a team and the prisoners retrieve the ball, they can throw it at the opposing team (from behind), but must not step out of prison while throwing. If a prisoner strikes an opposing player, she leaves prison and rejoins her team, while the struck player goes to prison (a net exchange of two players).

If the gym or field is too wide to contain the game, out of bounds should be established. All balls going out of bounds are awarded to the team (or prisoners) where the ball went out. Players cannot violate the center or prison lines to retrieve balls or dodge being hit except if there are no prisoners.

Teacher's Guide

Pris meets many needs because it has cooperating, competing, risking and strategy. Every time I lead it, the players do not want to stop playing.

* See *Game Kit* information on page 153.

Some players tend to dominate the play because of their throwing prowess, and terrorize weaker players. For safety reasons, you should set limits as to where players can be hit with the ball. Below the armpits is a good choice. Team strategies can be formulated to include all players regardless of their skill level and more democratically decide who throws the ball at whom. The game has an ebb and flow quality which is exciting—a team can be down to a few free players and still come back to win.

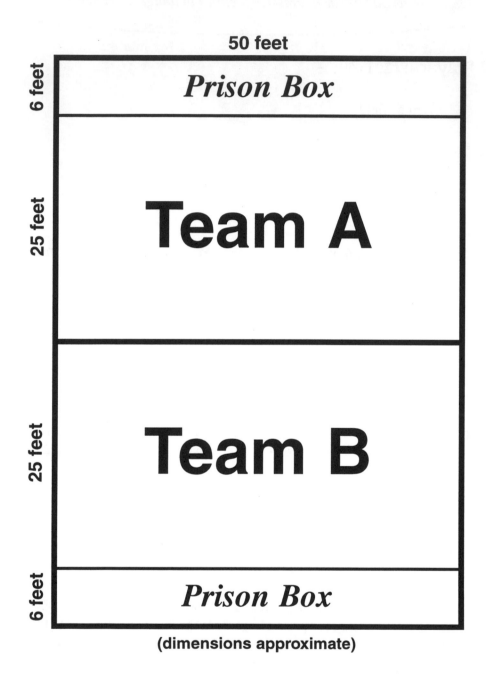

Quick Draw

Objective
To increase creativity and nonverbal communication skills.

Number of Players: Up to six teams of six to ten members.

Place: Any

Equipment: A pencil, pen or marker and paper for each team.

Formation: Team clusters equidistant from leader.

Description: A team, nonverbal communication race game.

Action

Each team sends one player to the leader, who whispers an abstract word (evil, success, spiritual, opportunity, friendship, etc.) to all players simultaneously and they rush back to their respective teams and use pencil and paper to draw those things that they think will communicate the idea to their teammates. The team members guess out loud whatever they think the word may be. When someone on the team guesses the correct word, the artist rushes back up to the leader. The first team to do so wins a point. The first team to reach a preset number of points wins.

The role of the artist (*It*) should be rotated. Artists may not use letters or numbers but may use symbols like $, % and #. The artists are not to talk or make any sounds.

Teacher's Guide

Because words, both written and spoken, are the dominant forms of conveying ideas, students find this game challenging. Players are frequently frustrated because they feel they do not have artistic talent. Some become self-conscious of their stick figures, stop sketching and start gesturing with their hands, turning the game into charades. On the other hand, players often realize that they have clever teammates and therefore become less pressured and more creative. When this happens the game reaches its highest level of enjoyment. I like this game because it challenges students to be disciplined as well as inventive. I mention discipline because some students will whisper the answer instead of drawing. Some groups can handle abstract words while others need more concrete ones. I usually ask winning artists to show their drawings to the entire group to stimulate ideas in others. I also encourage players to sketch more when I see them use pantomime because the gesturing bypasses the content of the game which is intended to develop the right-brain by use of symbols.

Quick Line Up

Objective
To teach organizational skills and cooperation.

Number of Players: 32 to 64

Place: Gym or field

Equipment: None

Formation: Four even teams, standing shoulder to shoulder, in a perfect square facing inward. The leader stands in the center.

Description: An active, competitive team game that requires organizational problem solving.

Action

One team always faces the leader, the second team is always on her right, the third team on her left, and the fourth faces her back. Each player must remember two things—his position relative to his teammates and to the leader. Each round of play begins when the leader rotates and comes to a stop. Then each team must reassemble into their original order and position relative to teammates and the leader. The first team to line up this way wins a point. The first team to reach a preset score wins the game. Players may not hold onto each other when moving.

Variation

If there is adequate space, the leader may move to a new spot in addition to rotating!

Teacher's Guide

Quick Line Up is rich in social content. It contains active and passive involvement, body contact, team spirit, cooperation, strategy, good natured rivalry, chaos and order. The intensity of the play can put strong pressure on the leader. She must be a fair and resolute judge who awards points despite objections from players. I usually recruit volunteers (extra players) to help judge which team wins each point.

A practice round without scoring is highly recommended because players cannot visualize how difficult it is to orient themselves in three dimensional shifting patterns, nor are they able to foresee how rough and determined other teams can be.

The rules do not address the issue of what teams can do to opposing players in route and I never mention whether it is legal to detain players from other teams. To do so may cause the action to become too rough. However, no matter what style of play *Quick Line Up* takes, it never fails to generate a great deal of enthusiasm and fun.

Quick Numbers

Objective
To improve concentration and mental discipline.

Number of Players: 12 to 25

Place: Classroom

Equipment: Chairs for all.

Formation: Circle, sitting in chairs.

Description: The most cognitive of a family of games where there is forced player response linked to a tempo, and any hesitation or failure to respond is penalized.

Action

Players are numbered consecutively around the circle, skipping the number four. *There is no number four!* The number one player always starts the game by calling the number of another player. This player must immediately call the number of another player, and so on. A player fails if he either hesitates, stutters or mispronounces, laughs, calls his own number, answers out of turn, or calls four! At this point the game stops, the erring player gets demoted to last seat as all the players behind him move down a chair. The numbers belong to the chairs, so when players move they must assume their new number. After all players learn their new numbers, the player in chair number one restarts the game for another round.

The object of the game is for every player to strive to become number one by not making any errors.

Teacher's Guide

Quick Numbers is an absorbing, intense game. The tension comes from having to control and pay attention to one's thinking and to others' cues, and it is just that combination of functioning that makes this a great game. Players who need relief can find it quickly by making an error thus becoming the last player.

Overall, *Quick Numbers* can hold students' attention for extended periods of time and is one of the few games in the *Social Play* repertoire that can be played without a leader.

Quick Numbers highlights some scintillating characteristics about brain functioning. You will observe players say, "four" (the most glaring mistake), look oblivious for a moment, and then put their hands over their mouths and scream, "Oh, No!" They will act like *two separate people*—one unaware for a split second of what the other says. My theory is that the nonverbal, right side of the brain usurps the speech center from the verbal left side, and says, "Four!" I think this takes place despite the fact that the game's rules speak exclusively to the left brain. But the competition, the ego, and the fear of failure are in the left domain of the brain. I speculate further that the right brain loves playing games and having fun and that it becomes bored of the left brain's intellectual, static role and takes over when it can to have fun! After all, laughter and moving to another chair is a right-brained, three-dimensional, motor activity. What's your theory?

Rescue Relay

Objective
To provide a cooperative experience with motor activity.

Number of Players: 20 to 50

Place: Gym or field

Equipment: None

Formation: Single file teams standing at the start line, with the number one players standing opposite from their teams at the finish line.

Description: A cooperative relay race game.

Action

The first runner for each team starts from the finish line 40 to 100 feet away from the rest of the team. At the "Go" signal, they race up to the first team member in line, take his hand and race back to the finish line. The original runner remains at the finish line and the new runner races back to the team and takes the next player in line by the hand and they race back to the finish line. This procedure continues until all the players are lined up at the finish line. The first team reassembled at the start line wins.

Teacher's Guide

This is a *Social Play* relay, and it has more social content than a sports relay. Cooperative hand-holding is what adds the social element. A very fast runner may be impatient when coupled with a slower runner and they may be a slower pair than two mediocre runners who are cooperating. Success in this relay is predicated on cooperation and the tolerance of intimacy (hand-holding).

I use this relay to help girls and boys to be comfortable in touching without practicing sexual rejection. If the students are robust and competitive, they may be able to overcome this serious barrier to healthy activities and wholesome relationships among the sexes. Of course, the relay is good fun for homogeneous groups too.

Scavenger Hunt

Objective
To build friendly intergroup relations.

Number of Players: 20 to 80

Place: Any

Equipment: Normal objects found on the players and in the playing area.

Formation: Team clusters, equidistant from the leader.

Description: A cooperative/competitive team scavenger hunt race game.

Action

Teams are randomly chosen and arranged in clusters, equidistant from the leader. Teams need only be approximately equal in number. Each team sends a player to the leader each round of the game. The leader whispers to these messengers the name of an object or objects that he wants brought to him. The messengers rush back to their teams, shout out the object(s) wanted, the team finds the object(s) and gives them to the messenger, who rushes them back to the leader. The first team to get the requested object(s) to the leader wins a point. The first team to reach a preset score wins. A new messenger is selected for each round.

When players serve as messengers they may not hand the leader objects from their person. They have the option, however, of leaving personal objects with the team before coming up to the leader.

Variations
See ***Bird, Beast And Fish*** and ***Quick Draw***. The game may also be adapted to using old magazines and scissors, the leader asking for certain ads or pictures.

Teacher's Guide

Scavenger Hunt never fails to arouse the interest and enthusiasm of students. It is a near perfect blend of competition and cooperation and this combination releases abundant interactive energy. Groups come alive when playing *Scavenger Hunt*.

If playing outdoors, you may use natural objects. Call for clover, grass, pebbles, dead insects, etc. It is sometimes appalling how brutally clever some players are. They will catch an insect, bring it to the leader, and when told they were asked for a dead one, they smack it and re-present it!

Scavenger Hunt is a game with strong social content. This means that it satisfies social interactive needs. It is a game that can be led and depended on to provide a successful *Social Play* experience. However, it does require good leadership technique, strong organizational command and control. There are many, many interactions and stimulations taking place in large multi-team games like this one.

Singing Geography

Objective
To provide a creative format for attention getting.

Number of Players: 20 to 30

Place: Any

Equipment: None

Formation: Circle, standing, the *It* leaving and returning to the playing area.

Description: A musical geography guessing game.

Action

Volunteer *It* leaves playing area while the group selects a place (country, town, city, etc.) and a well-known tune. Each player, in order, around the circle takes a syllable in the name of the place chosen. When the *It* returns, all players sing their one syllable to the tune. The *It* roams around listening and has three guesses to name the place. A new *It* is chosen for each round.

Teacher's Guide

In this game the players seem to be against the *It*, but are actually helping her and when the *It* guesses correctly, all players share in the joy.

Sometimes you can hear the word stand out from the din. It is a special musical moment when that happens—somewhat like seeing a rainbow.

Singing Hot And Cold

Objective
To foster group building through nonverbal communications.

Number of Players: 20 to 35

Place: Classroom

Equipment: None

Formation: Circle, sitting. The *It* leaves the playing area and returns to move anywhere in the playing area.

Description: A musical communication game.

Action

A volunteer *It* leaves the playing area, while the group decides two things. First, an action (for instance, untie someone's shoe) and second, a song to sing. When the *It* returns, the group sings the chosen song at varying volumes to help give clues to the *It* as to where to move and what to do. Loud singing denotes closeness to the action (getting hot) and quiet singing denotes being far from the correct action (getting cold).

Teacher's Guide

This is a creative communications game. When the group is confident and relating well, the actions accomplished can be quite intricate. This success rewards the group and the *It* with a feeling of fulfillment and lets them share the joy people have when relating and communicating well. However, a good leader does not allow the group to move too quickly towards the more complicated actions but guides the choices to the appropriate level of difficulty as the group becomes more experienced. Single actions like taking a player's glasses off are the best starters, while compound actions like taking the glasses off one player and placing them on a table can be done in later rounds.

The initial *It* usually feels that he is pitted against the group but after playing a few rounds the subsequent *Its* begin to trust the group's cues, and when successful, players will clap and cheer.

Steal The Dog's Bone

Objective
To teach appreciation of quiet and modulated sound.

Number of Players: 15 to 30

Place: Classroom or gym

Equipment:* A key ring with many keys (or several put together), and a blindfold.

Formation: A circle sitting on the floor, *It* blindfolded in the center.

Description: A sound detection challenge game.

Action

The leader arranges two signals: one to get the players to make loud noises and the second for instant silence. The *It* volunteers to become the dog, and sits in the center of the circle blindfolded. Next, the leader signals for noise, places the key ring (designated the "bone") somewhere close to the dog, and signals for silence and tiptoes out of the circle. (The reason for making noise is to keep the dog from hearing where the bone is placed.)

Players who want to steal the dog's bone raise their hands. The leader points to a challenger, and he attempts to move toward the dog's bone, pick it up and returns to his spot *without making enough noise to be detected by the dog*. If the dog thinks he hears a challenger, he points in that direction and says, "Bow wow!" If the dog is pointing in the direction of the challenger, he is caught and must return to his place and another challenger is selected.

When a challenger successfully picks up the bone and returns to his place in the circle without being detected, the bone is "stolen" and another dog is selected. Players are not to make intentional distracting noises.

* See *Game Kit* information on page 153.

Teacher's Guide

Steal The Dog's Bone is intriguing to play and watch. Some players are stealthy while others are noisy—their joints pop and crackle and gives them away. Some students have superior hearing and pick up sounds others can't. Some have uneven hearing patterns, hearing well in front but not to the rear or sides, etc. Still others become overloaded when hearing sounds and become confused and panicky. But all manner of dogs instill a strong challenge for the circle of players.

This game should quiet even the noisiest class. I teach the making noise and getting silent part like "warming up" a radio station audience to applaud on cue. If done well, the resulting quiet creates an aura of sanctity that is rarely experienced by young people today.

As leader, never allow players in the circle to make intentional, distracting noises that give advantage to the challenging player (in *Social Play* it is important that the *It* is never intentionally made to feel victimized or put at an unfair disadvantage). It is not an even match if these noises are allowed against the dog. After all, the ears cannot differentiate sounds as the eyes do light—sounds blend into a single noise.

Steeple Chase

Objective
To provide controlled physical expression of aggression.

Number of Players: 25 to 30

Place: Gym or field

Equipment: None

Formation: Teams sitting in straight lines fanning out from the center like the spokes of a huge wagon wheel. One extra player stands on the perimeter.

Description: A vigorous team race competition game.

Action

The first *It*, who does not belong to any team, walks around the outer perimeter, stops and selects a team of choice by tapping the last player on the back. That player taps the player in front of him and so on down the team until the first player is tapped. The first player stands up followed by the rest of the team. This first player determines which direction the team and the *It* will run around the formation. He can feign either way, then run out and around the outside of the formation with players and the *It* following or passing him (looks just like a steeple chase). All running players jockey for position, trying not to be the last runner to arrive 360 degrees around the formation into the original place sitting down. The last one back is *It* and the game repeats. Runners must not jump over, cut through, or touch seated players as they circle.

Teacher's Guide

This game challenges one's competitive drives and sense of survival. Even if not played deliberately aggressive (pushing, elbowing or tripping), it requires resolve and stamina. Sometimes a team is picked several times in a row and exhaustion takes its toll on the players who are not in good physical condition, especially when played in the hot sun or on an uneven grass field. All the above comments support the fact that this game appeared in Army recruit training manuals.

In spite of its rough, vigorous style, **Steeple Chase** is definitely a rich social game. It highlights many personality characteristics—the tough, rough, fast runners who want to be first in line, the players with competitive morals who will elbow and trip other players without blinking, and the slower running players frightened for their lives, trotting along last in line gingerly stepping over faster runners who went down in a fall. These characteristics provide fascinating entertainment for the inactive players.

The running in this game is hard on the ankles because of the constant circling, and fast players may slip on damp grass. Make sure the playing area is safe as possible.

Stride Ball

Objective
To provide outlets for anger and aggression.

Number of Players: 10 to 25

Place: Any

Equipment:* A playground ball or foam volleyball.

Formation: Circle, standing, legs spread in straddle position, feet touching the feet of adjacent players.

Description: A mock goal-tending ball game.

Action

A player must get a ball to go through another player's legs but tries to prevent it from going through hers. Hands must be held over the shins or above the knees *until* the ball actually comes (to prevent constant goal tending). Players cannot move their feet or block the ball with their legs. When the ball passes through a player's legs he is given a letter and must retrieve the ball and start play by rolling it across the *center* of the circle and not through the adjacent player's legs. The ball must remain on or near the ground and not hit the player's faces. Play continues until one player gets all the letters.

Teacher's Guide

Stride Ball was originally an elimination game. Elimination is not generally a worthy trait for *Social Play*. The elimination element is removed by assigning letters each time the ball goes through someone's legs. When a player accumulates the letters to spell a predetermined word (for example, E-N-D) the game ends! You may use S-T-O-P if you want a longer playing time.

This game can be very vigorous and the leader must caution players not to hit the ball up at faces. Instruct players not to hit the ball if it's high in the air, simply grab it and bring it back down to the ground.

Many players will be content with batting the ball away from themselves while players like myself like to play tough and will terrorize adjacent opponents with swift attempts at stuffing the ball between their legs. But I pay a price for this aggression—I invariably become the villain, and even if by a *lucky* quirk, the ball goes through my legs, it usually elicits a roar of approval.

* See *Game Kit* information on page 153.

Swat

Objective
To provide effective, fun outlets for anger and aggression.

Number of Players: 15 to 35

Place: Classroom or gym

Equipment:* Chairs for all, a rolled up, taped newspaper to swat with, and a empty waste basket.

Formation: Circle, sitting on chairs, inverted waste basket in the center of the circle.

Description: A continuous action tag (hitting) game.

Action

All players have a home base chair (they are never to sit in any other). The first *It* takes the swat in hand, goes up to another player, swats him *below* the waist, runs up and places the swat on the waste basket, and races to his chair. The swatted player chases, picks up the swat, and tries to hit the *It* (below the waist only) before the *It* reaches his chair. If the swatted player succeeds in swatting the *It*, he must return the swat to the waste basket and get into his seat before the *It* swats him back.

Whenever the chaser fails to swat the *It* before the *It* gets to his seat, the chaser becomes the *It* and chooses another player to swat and so on. There is no time to savor a successful swat, because pursuit should be immediate and continuous. If a swatter fails to place the swat on the basket and it falls to the floor, untouched by the pursuing player, all the players signal by saying, "Wooooooooo!" This signals to the swatter that he must return to the waste basket and replace the swat *while the pursuing player waits at the waste basket to swat him back!*

Teacher's Guide

Swat is one of my favorite games and it becomes *the* favorite of nearly every student that plays it. As a *Social Play* game it is richly interactive and loaded with useful social content. The central element in *Swat* is the free reign it gives to the expression of hostility and aggression in its corporal form. It is difficult to find socially acceptable outlets for these feelings in every day life but *Swat* provides it in a way that is fun in the bargain. The aggression is active, obvious and intentional, but not personal.

* See *Game Kit* information on page 153.

Why is the expression of hostility and aggression so important? Because everyone has these feelings in our culture (including students) and if denied proper outlets it surfaces either openly or passively in destructive ways. Vandalism, graffiti, fighting, lack of respect for teachers, are all prevalent manifestations of anger, hostility and aggression felt by masses of young people.

Human anger has Jekyll and Hyde qualities. The unfortunate characteristics of these feelings are:

1) It can become generalized and chronic.

2) It can add up and intensify.

3) It can be misdirected, and be disconnected to the persons or situations that caused it.

4) And it can be triggered and unleashed at unpredictable times and place.

These qualities taken together spell trouble for people whose lives give them reasons to have angry feelings. But the picture isn't all bleak because there is one quality of human anger that allows a nondestructive solution. That quality allows anger to be constructively dealt with, and dissipated through a broad range of activities. Listed in decreasing order of effectiveness (as seen by the author) they are: play, dramatics, aerobic-motor activity, sports (if coaches don't encourage antisocial attitudes), delaying reaction (counting to ten), social discussion, and one-on-one discussion. I find that nonsocial forms of violent expression, like kicking or punching inanimate objects, virtually useless. The verbal forms of dealing with anger are the weakest, especially when used with young children.

> **Note**
> The author finds that most adolescents have not developed a sense of humor but have become sadistic—meaning they laugh at the *pain* of others! To see what I mean, go to a Hollywood movie of the Schwarzenegger/Stallone genre and see what they laugh at—it's generally when someone is kicked in the groin.

When you lead *Swat* you will see the extent to which students have angry feelings. You will see some students hit very hard and you will hear others cheer when it happens. As the leader, you must remain alert to prevent the anger from becoming *real*, that is, directed towards specific individuals. I always encourage the *It* to pick someone quickly, which helps to ensure a random and not a personal selection. This technique also speeds up the action and increases the fun.

Adolescent groups generally hit harder than most other ages. You may have to end the game if players tend to hurt others, or you may pause and raise the issue of whether classmates want to have fun or hurt people. No matter how the game is played or ends, it should be a helpful experience in dealing with this volatile human emotion. If your students are generally burdened by angry feelings (rough neighborhood, special education emotionally disturbed, etc.) you must maintain a socially acceptable level of play. In such cases, *do not use huge, heavy swats, and do not lose control!*

Swedish Baseball

Objective
To learn names.

Number of Players: 12 to 30

Place: Classroom

Equipment: None

Formation: Seated circle

Description: A name game.

Action

The name of this game, *Swedish Baseball,* signifies a human head (attached, of course!). It is "thrown" by placing both hands on it and pretending to direct it towards a player whose name is called (you must know their name). That person "catches" the baseball by putting both hands on her head and then throwing the ball to another named player. The throwing and catching part can be dramatically exaggerated.

Teacher's Guide

This is a good game for a group to learn most members' names. The leader should start the play because she probably knows someone's name. Some people are shy and are stilted in throwing the *Swedish Baseball*. Others get very involved and act like professional baseball players catching balls thrown so hard that they fall back in their seats!

The Parlour Game (Charades)

Objective
To provide positive attention and self expression.

Number of Players: 16 to 35

Place: Classroom

Equipment: Paper, pencils, scissors, two containers (hats) and a watch with a second hand.

Formation: Two teams sitting on opposite sides of an acting area.

Description: Dramatic team game with pantomime communication element.

Action

Preliminary Action (10 minutes)
Teams move to separate areas and jot down titles of movies, books, songs, or plays (game can be restricted to only one category, if you wish). the titles are then cut into separate strips, one title each.

Main Action
Teams assemble in the playing area and one player from the first team picks a title strip from the second team. The player reads the title and makes sure he knows what it says and what the category it is in. When sure, he is given a maximum of two minutes to get his team to guess the correct title *without making a sound.* Teammates shout out what they think the acting player means by using a brainstorming style. The player may act the entire title, do individual words, or attempt to act out syllables. The time score is recorded and the second team sends a player to select a title from team #1, and so on. This continues until all players have a turn or until all titles have been performed. The team with the lowest time score wins. When this game is played frequently, an extensive sign language can develop but it is sufficient for beginners to know the following signals:

- A stylized pantomime of filming with a movie camera, opening a book, opening the mouth like a singer, and simulating stage curtains rising are quick ways to let the team know the category.

- The number of fingers held up equals the number of words in a title.

- Fingers are placed on the forearm to indicate the number of syllables.

- A tug at an ear means "sounds like."

- An index finger and thumb held out means a small word (such as "the," "it," "to," "and," "but," "so," "if," etc.)

- Pointing to a teammate means a correct guess (this is also accompanied by a shaking of the head indicating "yes") and the game may then proceed to the next word, syllable, etc.

- A player makes the motion of making a circle with his arms to signify that he will attempt to act out the entire title.

- A frown means the team isn't close and is on the wrong track.

- Enthusiasm shows that the team is close to the meaning.

- Players may not pantomime actual letters making up a word.

Teacher's Guide

This game used to be a popular parlour game. It even ended up as a television game in the fifties and sixties. When I lead this game, I'm often surprised by how many people have never played, and more importantly, how difficult it seems to be for people to perform in front of teammates. I therefore use lower level pantomime games to help prepare people to risk acting in front of others.

Thread The Needle

Objective
To help students to be comfortable with intimate proximity.

Number of Players: 15 to 60

Place: Gym or field (large space)

Equipment: None

Formation: Even teams of five or six holding hands standing in a line.

Description: An active, cooperative team competition game.

Action

Each team numbers their players consecutively. For each round, the leader calls out two consecutive numbers and those two players quickly raise their hands to form an arch. The two end players on each team rush through the arch turning the team inside out to its original order. The first team to return to their original order wins the point. Players may not drop hands. The first team to reach a preset score wins.

Teacher's Guide

This is a competitive team game that requires intimacy (hand holding) and cooperation. There is competition between teams and cooperation in the team. It is impossible to do well if players bicker or drop hands.

Thread The Needle is difficult to judge. Be prepared for disputes if group members feel strongly about winning. But the fun of watching the teams (they can get confused) compensates for having to be a judge.

Tire Pull

Objective
To provide energetic, safe outlets for aggression.

Number of Players: 12 to 24

Place: Gym or field

Equipment: An old tire.

Formation: Two opposing teams in parallel lines facing each other. Teams must be in an ascending size order, the smallest on one teams stands opposite of the largest of the opposing team. Distance between teams varies according to how energetic the players are. The tire is placed in the center.

Description: A more physical variation of **Steal The Bacon** where a tire is substituted for a cloth. The game has a tug-of-war element.

Action

Players are numbered consecutively in their teams starting at opposite ends so there will be two players with the same number, roughly of the same size standing diagonally across from each other. The leader shouts out a number and those two players rush out, grab the tire and attempt to pull it across their team's line (line is imaginary or drawn). The player who succeeds wins a point for his team. The leader may call additional numbers some times (especially if there is either a mismatch or a stalemate).

Teacher's Guide

This is a highly competitive physical game, and it can cause some players to feel embarrassed when defeated. Because the active players are the center of attention there is both negative pressure, due to the audience watching one lose, and the positive pressure of teammates cheering encouragement. If the team members are friendly and supportive, it is not ego-deflating for the one who is unsuccessful, but if the team is loaded with bad losers and those who scapegoat, one can suffer from a diminished self-confidence.

The issues in this game are similar to those in **Broom Hockey**.

Touch

Objective
To provide intimate proximity.

Number of Players: 12 to 35

Place: Any

Equipment: None

Formation: A cluster milling around the leader.

Description: A simple tactile mixer game.

Action

Leader names something and the players touch it. Players can touch as much as they want, using one finger or two hands. Players are free to move about.

Teacher's Guide

I have put his ultra-simple game to heavy-duty use for many years. As a closure activity it can bring a group together at the end of a *Social Play* session beautifully.

Often after explaining the game, a player will ask, "Can I touch myself?" I say, "Why touch yourself when you have so many others to touch?"

With older students, sexual joking usually occurs during this game. Sometimes at the start of the game players give out a mischievous chuckle while looking to me as if I'm a lecherous opportunist. But I never go past the comfort level. As a matter of fact, here is the usual rundown of the things I suggest to touch—you be the judge: a color, leather, metal jewelry, a fabric, a person (tallest, smallest, leader, etc.), a shoulder or two, a knee, a smile, hands, etc. What the leader must do is start out in an nonthreatening manner and move up to things that are more intimate. With younger students, colors and textures can be educational while older students focus more on the need to be touched.

I frequently end *Touch* by having all the players touch all the hands in a big circle and doing a rousing team cheer with hands raised high!

Twenty-One

Objective
To provide outlets for aggression.

Number of Players: 20 to 40

Place: Gym or outdoors

Equipment:* One 8.5" ball.

Formation: Circle, *It* in the middle.

Description: A one-against-the-world, counting game.

Action

The *It* throws the ball to anyone in the circle and the group loudly chants, "One!" The player receiving the ball then passes the ball to *either* neighbor and the group chants, "Two!" and so on. The passers may not pass the ball behind their backs, turn completely around, nor throw the ball to anyone besides either the right or left neighbor. The *It* has to knock the ball to the ground before the circle gets to "21." The circle "wins" if they get to "21" and the *It* wins if she knocks the ball down before "21."

If the *It* wins, she trades places with the player who lost the ball. If the circle wins, the *It* can be given another turn or a new *It* chosen.

Teacher's Guide

Twenty-One is useful for warming up a group to cooperate and function without hostility (**Guard The Chair** is another such game). It's a good blend of attention getting, aggression and working together.

This game pits one player against the world (the circle). Is it a fair match? What happens to a person's ego when they lose to the weakest possible opponent? It's devastating! What happens to self-esteem when you lose to the absolutely best opponent? It's not so bad, especially if you win some points; you can brag about those few, small victories. So in *Twenty-One*, it shouldn't bother anyone if the group gets to "21." The circle will love it!

* See *Game Kit* information on page 153.

Up Jenkins

Objective
To provide group trust and a feeling of esprit de corps.

Number of Players: 12 to 20

Place: Classroom or lunch room

Equipment: A quarter, a long table (or several tables placed end to end) and chairs.

Formation: Two teams sitting opposite at a long table.

Description: A team coin passing guessing game.

Action

Teams flip a coin to see who goes first. The winning team gets the coin and places their hands under the table. They start to pass and *pretend* to pass the coin back and forth. When ready, the opposing team's captain says, "Up Jenkins!" The team passing the coin must bring their elbows up on the table with fists clenched, palms facing the other team and one player holding the coin. The captain now orders, "Down Jenkins!" At that instant every team member simultaneously slam their palms opened flat on the table. The object for the guessing team is to detect (by sound or other means) which hand the coin is under. The object for the coin team is to avoid giving evidence as to which hand the coin is under. Only the captain orders which hands will be turned over but solicits information from teammates to help make the judgments. Hands are eliminated one at a time and placed on laps until the coin is found. The captain's role should be rotated each round.

The game is scored by the elimination method. The guessing team tries to uncover all the empty hands before uncovering the coin. The team receives a score of zero if the last hand uncovered has the coin. If the coin hand is selected before all other hands are turned over, penalty points are awarded for each hand still down.

Each round is scored and the game continues with the teams reversing roles each time. The team with the least number of points wins.

Teacher's Guide

This is a game that absorbs the players' attention. Sitting closely around a table concentrates the focus and makes the game feel comfortable. There is quiet, tension, accusation, suspense and laughter. The action keeps the players involved except the players sitting at the far end who are sometimes neglected

135

because the coin doesn't reach them. So you may have players change position, if this is a problem.

Some players hold the coin without sharing; others can't wait to unload it. Some players slam the coin down hard and silently; others do it slowly and are discovered when a belated tinkle of the coin is heard. Many are saved by the distracting noise of jewelry.

The best episodes happen when good team synchronization results in every hand hitting the table simultaneously without making a sound!

Vegetarianism

Objective
To focus positive attention on individuals.

Number of Players: 15 to 60

Place: Classroom or gym

Equipment: Chairs for all but one.

Formation: Sitting in a circle of chairs. The *It* stands in the center.

Description: A chair-for-all-but-one mixer game. In the family of ***A Big Wind Blows, Come Along, How Do You Like Your Neighbor?*** and ***Fruit Salad***.

Action

Each player must secretly choose and keep the vegetable they hate the most. The *It* player tries to get someone else's seat by either calling two or more vegetables or ***Vegetarianism!*** When she calls individual vegetables, those players whose vegetables she called must get a new seat and this is when the *It* tries to gain a seat. When she shouts ***Vegetarianism!*** every one must get a new seat! This is also a chance for the *It* to get a seat. The player left without a seat is the new *It* and starts the next round of play.

Teacher's Guide

Players should be reminded not to respond until the *It* has finished calling all their vegetables so as not to give themselves away.

The author 'invented' this variation of these important attention getting games because the need is so great among children who find themselves in large classes and don't have a home where adults are present to give them lots of attention.

It is good practice to follow ***Vegetarianism*** with a *go around* where each player gives their first name followed by their vegetable as their last name. You may get some great laughs because of the funny sounding names and relations.

Wave The Ocean

Objective
To supply outlets for aggression and provide intimate proximity.

Number of Players: 15 to 40

Place: Classroom or gym

Equipment: Chairs for everyone.

Formation: Sitting in a closed circle, chairs touching. The *It* stands in the circle.

Description: A one-against-the-group competition game.

Action

It stands in front of an empty chair and says either "wave the ocean right," or "wave the ocean left." If he says "right," the player to the left of the empty chair moves to his right into the empty chair and the other players in turn move to their right when the chair next to them becomes empty. The *It* then tries to sit in the vacant chair before a waving player does. If successful, he is no longer *It* and the player who should have moved into the vacant chair is *It* and stands up to start another round.

The *It* may change the direction of the wave at any time by saying, "wave the ocean left, right, left, right..." Players may not move unless the chair next to them is empty.

Teacher's Guide

Wave The Ocean is a difficult game to problem-solve. The *It* feels like there is a conspiracy against him. But the circle players are feeling just as desperate in trying not to be *It*. Some players think that they have the game figured out only to be constantly rebuffed and ending up on laps or on the floor. The *Its* can feel so overwhelmed that they fail to use their power to change the direction and confuse the waving players. They also get confused because their left direction is the circle's right!

Wave The Ocean has a contradictory content and form. It is both competitive and intimate. This factor makes it a game that players needing intimate proximity can receive it without being self conscious about it. Many preadolescent and adolescent youth find it difficult to show nonsexual physical affection to peers, and *Wave The Ocean* helps provide natural ways for them to get it.

This game ranks high in social interaction.

Who Am I?

Objective
To foster thought provoking mixing.

Number of Players: 20 to 40

Place: Classroom

Equipment: Slips of paper to be taped on every player's back. (Self-sticking typing labels work best.)

Formation: Random

Description: A famous person guessing mixer game.

Action

Names of famous persons living or dead are written on pieces of paper and placed on every player's back without that player seeing who she is. Then the players roam around asking other players yes-and-no-answer questions to learn clues about their mystery person attached to their backs. "Am I a male?" "Am I alive?" "Am I a musician....a painter?" Etc. When a player correctly guesses his famous person, he transfers the label to his chest. The game continues until all players correctly guess or the last few are told if they can't guess.

Teacher's Guide

An interesting mixer because its cognitive tasks help students be less self-conscious in approaching others. The famous people can be chosen from current history or social studies units. It is also a plus to witness the pride players show on their faces after they are successful.

Zip Zap!

Objective
To focus positive attention and to learn names.

Number of Players: 15 to 35

Place: Classroom

Equipment: Chairs for all but one.

Formation: Sitting in a circle with the *It* standing in the center.

Description: An-odd-person-out (musical chairs play element) name game.

Action

Each player learns the name of her Zip (the person on her right), and the name of her Zap (the person on her left). The *It* approaches any player, points and says, "Zip?" (or "Zap?") and counts to ten as fast as possible. The chosen player must say the name of her neighbor on her right before the count of ten. If she succeeds, she is safe and the *It* remains *It*. If she fails, she becomes *It* and switches places.

The *It* may, however, point to a player and say, "Zip Zap!" This means that every player must find a new seat while the *It* tries to get a seat so as not to be *It* again. The player without a seat is the new *It* and the game continues by everyone getting the names of their new Zip and Zap.

Teacher's Guide

This version of an attention getting game has a bonus feature—it helps students learn names. This is very beneficial when school starts.

Much of the humor in **Zip Zap!** derives from people's inability to function under social and time pressures. Most players become befuddled when trying to do the 'simple' task of remembering and saying someone's name. But as the game goes on they get better and the *It's* have to rely more on "Zip Zap!"

I like it best when I sit between a Lisa and a Lisa!

Appendix

What The Children Say—Letters To The Author

The following examples of letters to the author show what the children teach us about their *Social Play* experience in school. (Emphasis added by the author.)

Dear Mr. Aycox:

Thank you for coming every day you did come, and teaching us all the games you did. But I hope you're not so busy that you can't come anymore. Please will you try to come some Monday, Wednesday or Friday and have fun with us. *I'm sure we'll be much happier than.* So please come, please.

Sincerely, Everett

I want to thank you for coming to our class and working with us. *I think everybody in our class likes for you to come.* So please keep coming to our class. Cause if you don't on Friday afternoon our class will be sitting around doing work when we could be working with you.

Your Friend

I would like to thank you for coming. And I think we all should give you our appreciation for what you have done. *I think you are the best person I have ever seen.* I am begging you to come every Friday. "Please come!"

Love, Anthony

Thank you for coming to our class and working with us. I hope you are never too busy to come to our room. *You are the nicest man that I have ever played a game with.* I enjoy playing games with you.

Your friend, Sterling

I thank you for coming and playing lots of fun games. We have enjoyed you here. And I hope you don't leave us. Please try to keep coming in most of your spare time. ***I think if you didn't come we would be very sad and would not have a lot of fun.*** We like cooperating with you.

Sincerely, Sheila

I really hope you stick with us because we like you so much. We like you coming in our room. When you come we all yell. That's our proof that we like you. Do you like us? We like you. ***I hope we all like each other.*** Every time you don't come we get sad. Which you never did miss a day. And I hope you never do miss a day. I appreciate you coming here and teaching us all those games.

Love, Cynthia

Thank you for coming to our class and we like playing your games. The children like your games so much that they sometimes play them. ***Yesterday it was a fire drill and we were the best class outside. Because all of the classes were jumping up and down talking to each other. We were out there for a long time. Our line was nice and good. Our teacher treated us to ice cream.*** Thank you for all you have done for us.

Keven

Yesterday when Mr. Aycox was here I had fun in these games because the last game ***no one agreed and it was a terrible mess.*** I thought that we were going to have an assembly. But when I got in from recess I seen desks moved and the big circle of chairs. I know that we were going to have a lot of fun. I could not wait till Mr. Aycox got here because he is nice because I seen him and talked with him that's how I know. He was a nice man but he did not tell me nothing about coming to our room.

Nadine

I think it was fun because we played games and they were fun. The first game we played was do you like your next door neighbor? I like all the games we played. I think that he was a nice guy. I hope he comes back again next year. I think everybody like him but it's all I know I like him very much. I'm glad he came in to play games with us. He's a very nice guy. ***There wasn't one thing that I didn't like about him.***

Donald

I liked yesterday because I had fun. I learned things like how to play some games and a joke. I got mixed up when we played Wave The Ocean. It was fun when we played How Do You Like Your Nieghbor? I particularly like Swat because I didn't get swatted at all. We played El Tigre which was very fun *because I learned some different names and faces.*

Jessie Jo

I liked yesterday cause I had fun learning. We learned about other peoples' birth, when they were born, and what they like other people calling us names. *I would like to have lots of friends at the end of the year. So let's get all together and play some games that will help us. Also not let us call other people names.* He was a good person and nice. Mr. Aycox has a beard and mustache. I also like black and gray and sometimes white. If he comes again I'll be especially good.

Chris

The first game I thought was neat. *I learned to be a good sport. I also learned that me and Ginger have the same birthday.* I played that trick on my mom. I also played one of the games with my mom. I learned that I'm a good team member. *I learned to cooperate with other people.*

(not signed)

I felt good I had lots of fun. I didn't know it would be so very much fun. Everybody was having fun. I liked when we played Wave The Ocean Left Or Right. I hope you come back again. *I don't know if you will come back because of our behavior.* I don't think it was funny when Mrs. (**teacher**) fell down because you wouldn't know what could happen. Everybody was laughing because the teacher fell. But it was fun and exciting. I think it was fun to learn new games and have fun. *That was the first time I had fun in the classroom. Because mostly it is boring.* Sometimes people got us in trouble. But we kept on playing and playing. He said he will stay till 2:00 but he stayed a little later. It was fun for him to come.

Shane

At first I thought he was going to yell at us because we were bad. I was happy that he didn't. I liked playing games. Mostly "Swat" then I'd get back at people I didn't like. I also liked "Neighbors" because now I know who other people like and don't like. When I went home and told my mom what we did, she said, "He's a sociologist" (**psychologist?**) *I couldn't believe it so I said, "He can't be, because he was*

playing games with us!" By the time we stopped arguing it was supper time. After supper I told my dad and by the time we stopped arguing it was 9 o'clock. I felt good about Mr. Aycox because I like to have fun with people, and I like people coming into our room to have fun with us. I learned how to play new games and how to cooperate with people and depend on them to do the right thing. I had a lot of fun *because I don't know that many games* and I learned some new ones. I like the joke he told. He was gentle on us. *He didn't even have to yell at us.* I hope he comes again sometime. I like him very much.

Jeff

I like it very much. It was a very nice experience. Yesterday afternoon I learned what good sports some of my classmates are. Also I learned new games and a very funny joke. (I told it to my mom last night and she cracked up.) My favorite of all the games was, Wave The Ocean. Yesterday I learned what teamwork can do, like my old saying teamwork can do anything you want it to do, anything. Also I learned who my real friends are, really are. Also from Mr. Aycox I learned what consensus meant. *My favorite part of the afternoon was when he asked us our names I really liked some of the replies people used. It was a funny afternoon.* I found out that in El Tigre if everyone doesn't cooperate if doesn't work out at all. Also in "do you like your neighbor" you should never be offended at what they say even if it is your best friend. That's what I learned.

(not signed)

I had a lot of fun and got along very good with everybody. I did not get mad at anyone. I learned how to play new games and so did the class and I hope he comes again. It was nice to have him here because when he had to go that was the sad part. It was also fun to ask him questions. The games were fun and I had a good day and maybe everybody else did too. I wish he could come here every day. I like when people come here. It was nice for him to come and it was exciting. *I wish he was my uncle and he could teach me all the games he knew and songs and poems and it was fun telling Mr. Aycox our names and birthdays and we had to tell him our full names and what year we were born.* I want him to come again. Mr. Aycox is nice to the whole class and it was fun.

Kim

I think it was very good thing to have. Because I learned a lot of things. I learned how to agree, cooperation and new games. I liked the games Swat, Wave The Ocean, or Find A Seat. Then we told Mr. Aycox our names and our birthday and what people do to make us mad. We played this game where you had to act like a man, tiger, or a gun. *I didn't like that as much because people didn't cooperate or agree but otherwise it was fun.*

Tina

I felt sort of mad when we played "swat" because the newspaper fell off of the trash can all of the time, but then I felt good because Pam the girl I hit, was so slow she couldn't catch me. I liked when we said our names so I could say something about the same girl, Pam. El Tigre wasn't fun because we all didn't agree on either man, tiger or gun. We just did what we wanted, and it was a big mess. I also liked to learn the new games. The hardest game was "Wave The Ocean." I thought since one of the boys didn't get hurt when he fell I thought it was funny. What I didn't like was Ginger the orange haired child's attitude about the one game. *I would have fun if some of the people would have had fun.*

Carmel

How did I feel when Mr. Aycox was here? I felt very good because we had a lot of fun. We all played and were good sports. What I did not like was the girl's changed what we were going to do in the game. And we got no point. *We acted like children and not like grown-ups.* We thought we should have it our way. We were very mad because we lost the game. We didn't agree to do the same thing. We did not listen. We pouted and pouted until all the fun was over. It was time for him to leave and we felt very sad. He tried to be good but we were not. And maybe that will tell us the next time he comes.

(not signed)

I felt happy because us kids are (en)titled to have a little fun. I'm glad he came in because I like when people come into our room. *I felt happy because sometimes kids go home and all we did was work work work.* All of the games were new and I'm glad because now I can teach my mom and my friends. My mom can teach the Girl Scouts and they can teach their friends and so on. Mr. Aycox is a good man at games. *He came in to let us have fun.* He sure made me have fun.

Justin

I felt good yesterday because Mr. Aycox came to have fun. *It is fun to have fun.* I liked "How do you Like Your Neighbor" game, the best. I like the joke he told us too. I told that joke to my mom and dad. I am going to tell it to everyone else too. When Mr. Aycox came he gave us a break from work. I liked Mr. Aycox and probably everyone in the whole school like him too. At first I didn't know what was going on but after awhile I knew I had fun. *Some people got a little carried away because this was new to them* but I didn't get carried away. I really had fun. *Mr. Aycox probably had fun too!* I hope he comes again.

(not signed)

I really liked having Mr. Aycox with us. I had a great time. I felt it was a fun thing to do. I felt that it was nice of him to come to play with the children. *I like all the games except one the last game we played because all the people didn't agree on what they should do.* The games I like best was Swat. It was really fun to me. I like the time when Mrs. (**teacher**) fell when we played Swat. It was very exciting when he came in because we didn't know what he was going to do. I knew about the desks because I helped put them where they were and the chairs too. It was fun when we introduced ourselves to each other, because they got to know when we were born and what aggravates us the most in school. *I felt embarrassed when he told us how good the kids in the Midwest were.*

(not signed)

When we played the games this year I thought it was the funniest thing since the whole year. *When you play with us you make the games more fun.* Mr. Aycox I think *when you come to our school you brighten things up and you make people be happy.*

(not signed)

Feelings: I think it was fun but some people started arguing. Some people said that they don't care if they win or not. I myself would love to win games. *I will hate to lose.* They said it is just a game.

(not signed)

I thought it was fun. "How Do You Like Your Neighbor" I thought it taught us a lesson. *Games are to have fun with. Not to beat up anyone or kill them. It taught me a lot in a fun way. I feel much better after this. I feel happy.*

(not signed)

What I thought about Mr. Aycox? I thought it was terrific. I especially like when we played How Do You Like Your Neighbor, and Names of countries and spelling races. *He made me relaxed and I liked myself and I had fun. I didn't like when a lot of people were pushing and punching, yelling, carrying on.* Mr. Aycox I like you for a special friend.

(note signed)

Out of all the games we played with Mr. Aycox, I mostly liked the one when you say if you liked or disliked, the person you were sitting next to. *The reason I like that one best is because it teaches people a lesson about saying it to someone.* I think Mr. Aycox is a very nice man.

(not signed)

I felt it was very nice of Mr. Aycox to share his fun. I also felt happy and gay. I hope he comes again next year. The game I like best was (How Do You Like Your Neighbor) I liked it because everyone knew when someone said I don't like my neighbor we all knew they were *playing. I didn't like the spelling game because my team lost.*

Janine

Mr. Aycox, I felt good when I got caught in the middle of "How Do You Like Your Neighbor." *I felt kind of dumb but I like it very much.* I write poems. Please read one.
Poem:
Skies are blue, The Children are gay
But when they see you they are all very, very gay.
Dreams may talk to you but boys and girls love.

(not signed)

I really like your games and I think that some of your games are really neat. And I saw some people acted hot headed. *And because our team was losing (John) was almost crying. I didn't like that because he was being a poor sport.* I'm looking forward to seeing you next year.

(not signed)

I feel very good inside because we had a lot of fun. It was special because we do not get to do that very often. I feel good that you can show us games. I show my friends these games. When we cannot go outside for recess, we feel good to have some fun. I felt like my classmates were not good sports when we lost that spelling game. I felt a little embarrassed when I lost that game where you had to find out what color was on their back. *I lost to a girl.* I hope you come back next year.

(not signed)

I feel that the games we played today *made most of us think about what a good time means.* And I think we had a good time playing the things we played. *A lot of kids like you because you teach very well.* Thank you for coming.

(not signed)

❤ ❤ ❤

....Usually we talk a lot when a visitor comes, but when you came it was fun.

(Nichole)

❤ ❤ ❤

....At first, when you came into the room, **I thought we were going to do something boring, but I changed my mind....**

(Your friend, Harry)

❤ ❤ ❤

....The games were so fun, **I forgot that we were learning at the same time.** It was fun cause we moved around and not sit there and just listen....

(Your friend, Zenith)

❤ ❤ ❤

....I guess you're right, sometimes you do have to get out and have some fun.

(Louis)

❤ ❤ ❤

....You were one of the best people to visit this class. The games *ruled,* they were the *bomb!*

(Your friend, Drew)

What The Teachers Say About *Social Play*

Some quotes from teachers' evaluation forms after attending an in-service led by Frank Aycox:

"All teachers could use it"

"It teaches the power of play"

"We need more help in this area"

"Can be used in any classroom"

"It is active and helps with ideas for the classroom"

"We've forgotten the purpose and value of play. Great!"

"Many applications for positive change"

"Learned A Lot — Nothing like this is taught to teachers!"

"Children need to be children and able to play."

"That we as teachers need to remember that play is so important to children's being."

"There must be a time to play, not just work."

"How refreshing to attend an inservice day that had so much to offer. Now I have a chance to be the best PE teacher in town!"

"Our students and teachers both had fun and benefited from your expertise. You have a unique way of dealing with children."

"I wanted to let you know that you had a profound effect upon the manner in which I interact with my students and they with me. I had good lesson plans, lots of enthusiasm, and a desire to give something to my students. I was overwhelmed by the social needs of my students. But, after hearing you speak and reading your book, things turned around — as if by magic!"

SUGGESTED READING

Boyd, Neva L. <u>Handbook of Games,</u> an authorized facsimile, Ann Arbor, Michigan: University Micro-films (A Xerox Co.), 1973

<u>Play and Game Theory in Group Work</u>, Chicago. University of Illinois Graduate School of Social Work, 1971

Bronfenbrenner, Urie. <u>Two Worlds of Childhood U.S. and U.S.S.R.</u>, New York: Simon and Schuster, 1970.

Cullum, Albert. <u>The Geranium On The Window Sill Just Died But Teacher You Went Right On</u>, Holland: Harlin Quist, Inc., 1971.

Any number of games books may contain a social game or other activity that could add to a *Social Play* session—you will have to judge whether it is suitable. Also feel free to adapt material to meet your specific situation. Good luck and good fun!

Index of Games

Classification Key

A = Anger/Aggression
C = Cooperation/Team Building
D = Dramatic
F = Focus Of Positive Attention
G = Getting Acquainted

H = High Energy
I = Intimate proximity
M = Musical
T = Thought Provoking

Game	*Classification*	*Page*
A Big Wind Blows	F-G	35
Airport	C-D-T	36
Alibi	D-T	37
Alphabet Race	C-T	39
Alphabet Volleyball	A-C	41
Balloon Burst Relay	A-C-F	42
Bird, Beast Or Fish	C-D-F-T	43
Broom Hockey	A-F-H	44
Bull In The Ring	A-C-F-H-I-T	45
Caboose Dodgeball	A-C-F-H-I	46
Catch A Smile	C-F-I-M	48
Chain Pantomime	D-T	49
Chosen	C-F-G-T	51
Circle Kho	C-F-H	52
Coffee Pot	F-T	53
Coin Relay	C-H-I	54
Colored Squares	F-H-I	56
Come Along	C-F-G-I-M	58
Dzien Dobry	F-I	60
Elbow Tag	F-H-I	62
El Tigre	A-C-D-I-T	64
Elephant And Giraffe	D-F-I	66
Fibbing	F-G-T	68
Fire On The Mountain	F-I-M	69
Front To Front	F-G-I	71
Fruit Salad	F-T	73
Go Around	C-F-G	75
Group Buzz	C-T	77
Guard The Chair	A-C-F-H	79
Guess The Leader	C-F-T	80

Game	*Classification*	*Page*
How Do You Like Your Neighbor?	A-F	81
Howdy Neighbor	C-F-I	83
Human Tic Tac Toe	F-T	85
I'm Going To California	D-F-G-T	87
I'm Thinking Of A Word That Rhymes With	D-F-T	88
In Plain View	F-T	90
In The Manner Of The Adverb	C-D-F-T	91
Jerusalem, Jericho	F	92
Jump Stick Relay	C-H	94
Kangaroo Relay	F-C	96
Last Couple Stoop	H-I-M	97
Lemonade	C-D-H-I	99
Line Tug Of War	A-C-H-I	101
Manito	F-G	103
Pass A Smile	A-C-I	105
Predicament	F-T	106
Pressure Nouns	F-T	107
Pris	A-C-H	109
Quick Draw	C-F-T	111
Quick Line Up	C-H-I	112
Quick Numbers	F-T	114
Rescue Relay	C-H-I	116
Scavenger Hunt	C-F-I	117
Singing Geography	C-F-M-T	119
Singing Hot And Cold	C-F-T	120
Steal The Dog's Bone	F-T	121
Steeple Chase	A-H-I	123
Stride Ball	A-H-I	125
Swat	A-F-H	126
Swedish Baseball	G	128
The Parlour Game (Charades)	C-D-F-T	129
Thread The Needle	C-H-I	131
Tire Pull	A-F-H	132
Touch	C-G-I	133
Twenty One	A-F-H	134
Up Jenkins	C-F-I-T	135
Vegetarianism	F-T-H	137
Wave The Ocean	A-F-H-I	138
Who Am I?	C-G-T	139
Zip Zap!	F-G-H	140

Contact the Author Direct
for
Game Presentations, Workshops,
and Consultations

write:
Frank Aycox
219 East Gowen Ave
Philadelphia, PA 19119

or
Phone: 1-215-247-4231
Fax: 1-215-247-0888

FREE
PUBLISHER'S CATALOG

Call toll-free or write for our free catalog of

INNOVATIVE CURRICULUM GUIDEBOOKS
AND
MATERIALS

for
Movement Education and Perceptual-Motor Development
(includes movement coordination equipment)

Call Toll-Free:
1-800-524-9091

or write:

FRONT ROW EXPERIENCE
540 Discovery Bay Blvd.
Discovery Bay, CA 94514-9454